☑ Check Your Lifestyle

by Knofel Staton

Putting Proverbs Into Practice

A division of STANDARD PUBLISHING
Cincinnati, Ohio
39997

DEDICATION

To Randy, Rena, Rhonda, and Rachel,
our children, who have taught us more than
any school could have

APPRECIATION

I have never written a book that is
entirely my own. For this book I am in-
debted to my wife, Julia, who gave valuable suggestions to the original manuscript
and typed it.

Library of Congress Catalog Card No. 78-66436
ISBN: 0-87239-233-3

PREFACE

It is so easy to settle down into the security of institutional religion by limiting our Christianity to the performing of correct rituals. We attend the services, read the Bible, pray to God, partake of the Lord's Supper, sing hymns, give our money, baptize the repentant, and teach the classes.

All of these are important, and should not be neglected, but they are not all-inclusive. There is much more to Christianity than the formal ceremonies and public performances. Christianity is effective only when it moves from the sanctuary to the street.

God keeps reminding us of this truth in His Word, and the book of Proverbs is an excellent example. We cannot read Proverbs without repeatedly coming upon some painfully practical teaching, for it translates Judean-Christian principles into the nitty-gritty of man's daily affairs.

But it is not enough just to study Proverbs, or even to share the wise truths of Proverbs. We must live them out! We must heed the word of caution that Jesus gave to His disciples about certain leaders of the day:

"Therefore all that they tell you, do and observe, but do not do according to their deeds; for they say things, and do not do them" (Matthew 23:3).

Solomon himself is a clear demonstration of this truth. He had the wisdom; he knew what was right; he shared the great truths with others; but he allowed "strange women" to lead him away from God's will (1 Kings 11:1-13). His son, Rehoboam, followed his father's example, not his words (1 Kings 12). It is only as we become absorbed in *obeying* these precious truths that our progress will be evident (1 Timothy 4:15). We must practice with our lives what we preach with our lips!

I have written this book to help you answer the all-important question, "What can I do to apply Proverbs to my life today?" I want you to be able to put Proverbs into practice. For this purpose I have selected some of the major topics of the book, related them to teachings of the New Testament, and made suggestions about really putting them into practice and making them part of your lifestyle.

At the end of each chapter I have included a section entitled "Just for Today." Try putting into practice the specific suggestions of each chapter, and continue doing so throughout the book. If the suggestions offered do not fit your specific situation, write your own application or adaptation of them. I recommend that you read one chapter of the book each day and put it into practice that same day. I also heartily recommend your reading a chapter from the book of Proverbs each day for the rest of your life. You will be greatly enriched for doing so.

—*Knofel Staton*

CONTENTS

Chapter One

Be Healthy God's Way *(Proverbs 3:1, 2)*

Unless Jesus comes first, the fatality rate for all of us is one hundred percent. Death has each one of us in its sight, and its aim is perfect. Given enough time, it will not miss us.

I doubt that any of us is intentionally urging death to come. We are living in a very health-conscious society. Health foods, health clubs, and health magazines are enjoying bumper sales. We are all interested in trying to prevent an untimely death.

This does not mean that we are faithless and are not longing for Heaven, but it shows that we appreciate how God has created our world. Solomon wanted his son to know how to prolong his life. God has an effective preventive medicine program that all of us can practice and benefit from. Solomon had insight into God's health program and shared it with his son, and with us. God's health program has much to do with our having positive attitudes and good speech habits. Before discussing these in detail, however, let us consider why God's program works.

The Harmony of Our Bodies

God has designed our bodies to be intricate connectional systems. Each part of our bodies is connected and cross-connected with every other part. We are blended together in harmony. When one part is off tune, the whole body's harmony is off. Everything is thrown off balance.

It is similar to dropping a rock into a stream. It is not only the exact spot where the rock hits that the water is disturbed. All the water gets disturbed. The ripples caused by the one rock extend even to the edges of the stream. What affects one part of the water affects all the water.

We are the same way. When I stub my toe, it is not the only part of my body that hurts. I am hurting all over. In fact, even before my brain knows the toe is hurt, the rest of the body is involved in helping the toe make compensations for the disruption. The toe sends a message to the brain through the nervous system, and the brain interprets the message as: "That toe was hit and is hurting." Then the mouth joins in and lets out an appropriate yell. The hand reaches down to hold the toe and seeks to soothe it. Every part of the body is off its normal routine. There are alterations in the beat of the heart and in the bloodstream. The whole body is in disharmony.

The very word "disease" points to the disharmony of the body. If we break the word into two parts, we have dis-ease, which means "not at ease," not at peace, not in harmony. When we are sick, the body is not at ease, but is dis-eased.

If we want to be really technical, we could say that each of us is a psychosomatic whole person. That is to say that the mind (psyche) and body (soma) are so related and interrelated that they affect each other.

At one time some Greek thinkers taught differently. They taught that a person was put together with entirely different and functionally detached parts. What we did with our bodies would not affect our spirits or souls, and vice versa. This philosophy is all wrong. Paul was correcting this type of thinking when he wrote:

"Now may the God of peace Himself sanctify you *entirely*; and may your spirit and soul and body be preserved *complete, without blame at the coming of our Lord Jesus Christ"* (1 Thessalonians 5:23).

We can understand how our bodies are in harmony as we analyze our daily experiences. Remember those times when your small child ran into the house with a hurt finger, crying as if death were at his door? You kissed the spot, and the cry turned into a sigh. What physical medicine was in that kiss? None. It was the touch of love that healed. It meant someone cared—and then the hurt was gone or at least deemed unimportant.

How about when you are sick? Do you want to be isolated and alone? Few people do. I don't. I want to be at home, in my own bed, and have my wife nearby. She may not give me any pills, but she gives me the medicine in God's health program: kind words, supportive companionship, positive attitudes, and love.

Have you ever awakened on a cloudy, gloomy day and immediately felt depressed? The weather does affect our emotions. High pressure affects our physical bodies, and at the same time our attitudes change. Put a person in a room with a temperature of 120° and see how soon his whole attitude changes. Our bodies and attitudes certainly are connected.

With this truth in our minds, let us now consider God's health program as told by Solomon to his son.

Live out Godly Teaching

Solomon did not make lists of detailed steps for good health to guide his son, but he spoke of broad, comprehensive principles. He said that living out godly teachings will add "length of days and years of life" (Proverbs 3:2). God's way of doing things will add peace to a person. As we have already discussed, peace is the opposite of dis-ease. When your mind is at peace, your body will be at ease.

Solomon told his son to practice kindness, truth (3:3), trust (v. 5), and humility (v. 7). Then he added that these "will be healing to your body, and refreshment to your bones" (v. 8). A godly life will allow your sleep to be sweet (v. 24). Good conduct is God's Sominex for all of us. Be good and sleep—peaceful sleep—sleep—sleep.

Solomon went so far as to say that godly teaching gives health and vigor to the whole body (4:22; 13:14). Years later, Paul echoed the same idea when he wrote to young Timothy. Paul, an aged man, wanted his young protege to enjoy a long life, so did he tell him to jog two miles a day and take plenty of vitamins? No, not quite. His advice was:

"Discipline yourself for the purpose of godliness; for bodily discipline is only of little profit, but godliness is profitable for all things, since it holds promise for the present life and also for the life to come" (1 Timothy 4:7, 8).

Watch Your Speech

Your talk can affect your stomach, said Solomon (Proverbs 18:20). We cannot speak angrily, excitedly, or anxiously without certain glands releasing juices into our stomach. Haven't you ever felt sick at your stomach after you spouted off in anger and said things you knew you shouldn't have?

If your mouth is dis-eased, your stomach will be thrown off balance.

Even doctors today tell us that many of our stomach troubles—ulcers, cancer, upset—are triggered and agitated by our unhealthy speech. To allow "sick" talk to come out of our mouths is like dumping garbage into our stomachs. Instead of picking up the Alka-Seltzer or Milk of Magnesia to get relief, perhaps we need to consider altering our speech habits. Guarding your words can help preserve your life (13:3).

James warned that when the tongue has been touched by Hell, it can defile the whole body and set on fire the course of life (James 3:6). The medicine from the pharmacy may treat the symptoms, but the preventive program of God treats the source of the problem.

Practice Joy and Tranquillity

Joy is good medicine (Proverbs 17:22). When a man is sad, anxious, or his spirit is broken (15:13; 12:25), his resistance to sickness lowers. He will get sick more easily. A happy heart will soothe and tranquilize like medicine. Solomon said:

"A tranquil heart is life to the body, but passion is rottenness to the bones" (14:30).

It is not enough to pop vitamin pills, jog every day, eat natural foods, and drink lots of water. Vitality comes from proper attitudes.

No wonder Jesus told the devil that man does not live by bread alone, but by every word that proceeds from God (Matthew 4:4). Obeying God's Word is one way to receive and keep joy. Jesus pointed that out when He said:

"These things have I spoken to you, that my joy

may be in you, and that your joy may be made full" (John 15:11).*

God does not want us to be sad or anxious. Joy is a fruit of the Spirit listed right after love (Galatians 5:22). Why do we forget that joy is to be an integral part of our Christian lives? We hear many sermons on love but very few on joy. I'm sure you have known some Christians who live as if joy were sinful.

Jesus preached His most memorable sermon on being happy, or "blessed" (Matthew 5:3-11), ending His introduction with the command to be glad and rejoice (5:12). Not only does He want us to enter into the *love* of our Master and into the *conduct* of our Master, but also into the *joy* of our Master (Matthew 25:21). Jesus came that we might have abundant life (John 10:10). God wants us to know that life is to be enjoyed, not just endured (Philippians 2:18; 3:1; 4:4; 1 Thessalonians 5:16; James 1:2).

Not only is it easier to get sick when our spirits are down, but it is harder to get well when we are sad or anxious. Our medical bills and our insurance could be reduced greatly if we took Solomon seriously:

"The spirit of a man can endure his sickness, but a broken spirit who can bear?" (Proverbs 18:14).

Doctors can tell you that a negative spirit will work as a counteragent to medical treatment. Many have told their patients, "You will never get well, unless you want to get well." The power of the mind is so strong that a person who keeps thinking he is sick will get sick. A major portion of the healing process is to *think* about getting well, even visualizing the healing of the part of the body that is affected. Thinking positively is a healing power as is faith.

Don't Worry

Worrying or daydreaming about unfulfilled desires can make you sick (13:12, 19). Haven't you ever got yourself tied up into knots worrying about something that never happened?

I am usually short of money at income tax time. If I am expecting a refund, I will worry and expect it to come each day, and spend it before I ever get it. We worry about so many things. Worry really is a waste of time and precious energy. Jesus said:

"Do not be anxious for tomorrow; for tomorrow will take care of itself" (Matthew 6:34).

We must remember as parents to avoid making promises to our children that we are not sure we can keep. We don't want to teach our children how to worry.

"Hope deferred makes the heart sick, but desire fulfilled is a tree of life" (Proverbs 13:12).

We must be cautious about making promises or about making them far ahead of time, but when a promise is made, we must be sure to carry it through.

God has kept His promises to us. He made many precious promises (2 Peter 1:4), and He has backed them up with the resurrection of Jesus. We are not a hopeless, anxious people. We know and trust that God will carry through. We have been born again to a living hope through Jesus' resurrection (1 Peter 1:3). That hope will become our eternal inheritance (1:4) and a final reality, then all sickness will vanish (Revelation 21:1-4).

A Word of Caution

Let us not go to extremes when putting God's health program into practice. Along with putting these principles into practice, we also need to utilize the advances of medical science and go to the doctor. We also must remember that death and sickness are inevitable. Our days are only a breath (Job 7:7). We are just a "vapor that appears for a little while and then vanishes away" (James 4:14). We may be here today, but gone tomorrow.

Some people teach that, since Jesus took our infirmities (Matthew 8:17), anyone who is really in Jesus will not get sick. They quote Deuteronomy 28:21-23 and suggest that these curses are the same as Abraham's curse from which Christ has redeemed us (Galatians 3:13). This teaching has made some Christians feel guilty because they get sick.

The curse from which Christ redeemed us is not sickness, but eternal separation from God. Timothy was sick often (1 Timothy 5:23), and Paul was sick and had no deliverance (2 Corinthians 12:7-10). God does not want us to think that we can avoid sickness and death altogether.

At the same time, we do not want to hasten sickness and death by ignoring God's health plan. He designed us and knows what benefits us. Give your life to Jesus and let Him give life abundantly to you. Then, and only then, will you have the power to put the proverbs of Solomon into practice.

JUST FOR TODAY

I will try to put God's health program into practice by being good, by being joyful, by watching my speech, and by not worrying.

Chapter Two

Manage Your Mind *(Proverbs 27:19)*

"Comb your hair, Randy."

"Rena, that top does not go with your slacks."

"Rhonda, don't forget to brush your teeth."

"Rachel, come here. Your face needs washing."

That's the way it sounds at our house before we leave for some activity. It is important that we teach our children how to be well-groomed and to be examples of good grooming ourselves. We must never forget, though, that what we look like on the outside does not necessarily reflect what we are on the inside.

"You can't tell a book by its cover" is a popular saying that applies to people also: "You can't tell a character by the coverings." What we really are, we are from the inside out. Of course, we are concerned about how we and our children *look* when we go somewhere, but are we just as concerned about what we and our children *think?*

Solomon wanted his son to know that what he thought was an instant replay of what he really was:

"As in water face reflects face, so the heart of man reflects man" (Proverbs 27:19).

In the Bible, the word "heart" refers to the "mind."

It is possible to look nice on the outside, but to

be an ugly, polluted mess on the inside. Some of the most well-groomed people are highly paid criminals. It is possible for a healthy-looking body to be eaten up with cancer. Jesus expressed this principle as He spoke to some of the people of His day:

" 'For you are like whitewashed tombs which on the outside appear beautiful, but inside they are full of dead men's bones and all uncleanness. Even so you too outwardly appear righteous to men, but inwardly you are full of hypocrisy and lawlessness' " (Matthew 23:27, 28).

The apostle Paul was disappointed in people who took pride in their appearance, but not in their hearts (2 Corinthians 5:12). How can one show pride in his mind (heart)? By properly grooming it.

The Mind Is a Computer
The mind is the most intriguing part of us. There is much about mentality that even researchers and scientists cannot tell us. Our minds are continually being fed data from the day we are born, affecting our conduct and who we really are. Just like computers, our minds do not "forget." Some data we can put into "cold storage" where it cannot be recalled under ordinary circumstances, but researchers tell us that our minds record and store everything.

Experiments using hypnosis prove that a mind can be forced back in time to recall minute experiences and facts. A person who is under hypnosis can be told to write his name as he did when he was five years old, and he will print it exactly as he did at that age. A person in a hypnotic state can be asked to speak as he did at three years of age, and he will do so. Under hypnosis a person can recall painful experiences that he does not remember under normal conditions.

The mind also stores data that we are not even aware we are absorbing. A group of people were asked to walk through a section of the library and look at the books on the shelves as they walked through. Later they were asked to write down the titles of as many books as they could remember seeing. Most of the group could recall only one or two; some could not remember any titles. They had not consciously intended to remember the book titles. Under hypnosis, their minds recalled every book their eyes had seen on the shelves.

Everything we see or hear or do goes into the mind, whether we intend for it to do so or not, or even when we are not aware that it is happening. People who work with mass media and in the entertainment fields are well aware of this truth, and use it to their advantage. Therefore, it is of utmost importance for us to be concerned about the things to which our own minds and the minds of our children are being exposed. Whatever goes into our minds has the potential of showing forth in our conduct and character.

Areas of the Mind

One area of the mind is what I call the "active duty" area. The thoughts in this area affect our conduct at any given moment. What you are thinking now is in this area.

Everything that the mind absorbs has the capacity to remain in this "active duty" zone and become an integral part of one's character. One can consciously determine what data will stay there and what will not. If we think on the data, speak about it and act upon it, it becomes a part of us.

In the West, the Oregon Trail can still be traced because of the deep ruts that were continually reinforced by the wagon wheels as the pioneers headed to new territory. Similarly, every time we reinforce a thought by meditating about it, speaking about it, and/or acting upon it, a rut is reinforced in our minds the same way as the ruts in the mud made by the wheels. What ruts are you digging into the active duty area of your mind? Be as concerned about that as Jesus was when He said:

" 'The things that proceed out of the mouth come from the heart, and those defile the man' " (Matthew 15:18).

The second area of the mind is what I call the "active reserve" zone. This is the transitional or temporary area. The thoughts in this area are not used daily, only occasionally. For instance, you may not look for the bad in other people as a normal way of life, but once in a while you do. It is like the active military reserves, equipped and ready to be used when called up. It is trained by usage just enough to remain "ready." The more usage these thoughts receive, the closer they move toward the active duty zone. With repeated call-ups, they will be transferred to the active duty area.

Area three is the inactive reserve or "cold storage" area. The data that our minds have taken in but don't recall are stored here. These thoughts do not affect our conduct or character unless they are somehow recalled and used, perhaps through severe emotional trauma.

Every piece of data the mind takes in comes initially into the active duty area, but we decide immediately where it goes from there. We either keep it in the active duty area, put it in the active reserve area, or we send it to cold storage. We could diagram it like this:

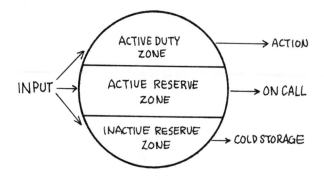

Mind Management

I suspect that many of you send the thoughts of most of the sermons you hear straight to cold storage. You don't intend to think about what you have heard when you get home. You don't intend to speak about it to someone else. You don't intend to allow it to change anything about your conduct. You are no different from the majority of people in this world. We all resist change. We don't like change, but change we must. Christianity began with the idea of change, as illustrated in the word "repent," and the Christian life continues to urge change, as seen in the words "obey, mature, be edified."

To have well-groomed minds, we must be committed to keeping good thoughts on active duty. That is why Paul wrote:

"If then you have been raised up with Christ, keep seeking the things above, . . . Set your minds on the things above, not on the things that are on earth" (Colossians 3:1, 2).

Reinforce the good thoughts by meditating upon them, speaking about them to others, and by putting them into practice. This was Paul's way:

"Finally, brethren, whatever is true, whatever is honorable, whatever is right, whatever is pure, whatever is lovely, whatever is of good repute, if there is any excellence and if anything worthy of praise, let your mind dwell on these things. The things you have learned and received and heard and seen in me, practice these things; and the God of peace shall be with you" (Philippians 4:8, 9).

We must also be committed to sending the bad data to the cold storage area. Paul told us to do so:

"Put to death therefore what is earthly in you: immorality, impurity, passion, evil desire, and covetousness, which is idolatry" (Colossians 3:5, RSV).

Paul meant that we should put bad thoughts into cold storage so they would not affect our conduct. This is what mind management is all about. We can and do manage our minds. We need to be aware of what we are putting into our minds and how our characters are affected. We need to determine that we will manage our minds as mature Christians should. We can send data to cold storage if we do not dwell on the bad thought, speak about it, put it into action, or continually enter an environment that will reinforce that thought.

We spend a lot of money supporting landfills to dispose of our garbage. We spend a lot of time, energy, and money preserving wildlife and scenic views. We speak loudly about cleaning up the atmosphere and water. But the land, air, and water are not as consistently and continuously assaulted by pollution as are our minds.

Where are those voices when mental garbage is openly dumped into books on the shelves and into films in the theaters? It is this kind of garbage that will decay and destroy us much more quickly and completely than the physical garbage of our kitchens!

Putting It Into Practice

1. *Feed your mind on godly teaching.* Actively seek to take in the proper data. We cannot expect to absorb good thoughts and experiences by accident. Solomon made it clear to his son that one needs to receive the teachings, be attentive to them, treasure them, incline the heart to them through discernment, and then seek, search, and ask for understanding (Proverbs 2:1-4).

Set a goal for reading the Bible and stick to it. Attend the services of your church regularly and *listen.* Take advantage of church conventions, clinics, and seminars. Subscribe to good Christian magazines. Read good, uplifting, spiritual books. Take a Bible corrrespondence course. Listen to good music. Fellowship with Christian people.

2. *Control the television set.* Don't let it control you. Turn it off when violence, dirty talk or sexual innuendos, and/or anti-Christian conduct is being displayed. Don't allow your mind to feed on that garbage. Remember those ruts that are being formed! Write to the television stations. Let them know how you feel about filth and violence.

3. *Control what you read.* Burn those vile books and magazines that crowd your bookshelves. Do not look at the "girlie" magazines at the store counters. Don't buy those gossipy periodicals. Many good books have been written through the years; fill your mind with them.

4. *Control what you hear.* Listen to good music, something that is uplifting, wholesome, or soothing. Don't fill your mind with filthy lyrics of some of the popular or "hard rock" songs. Listen to radio programs that can stimulate your thinking and educate your mind.

5. *Surround yourself with Christian friends.* Don't go to places where immorality is practiced. Stay away from beer and "pot" parties, and avoid clubs that feature dancing, gambling, and gossip. Don't be squeezed into the mold of the worldly society, just for the sake of being "in." Be transformed by the renewing of your own mind (Romans 12:2). What goes into our minds will be seen in our conduct and character. It is dangerous to become involved with the wrong people, unless you go prepared to witness for Christ, defend your faith, and win them to Christ.

May our minds be as well-groomed as our bodies!

JUST FOR TODAY

I will enrich my mind with what I read, see, and hear. I will remove anything from my environment that would not enhance my Christian life.

Chapter Three

Cool It! *(Proverbs 16:32)*

"Colonel, you shut up!"

The next day after I had uttered those words, and as I sat in the base commander's office, I decided that as a sergeant I would never say such a thing to a colonel again, especially if that colonel were the base commander.

It had been a busy day in the control tower of the airport in Korea. The bombers were coming and going at an unusually heavy pace. I was the supervisor in charge of the controllers, who were doing an excellent job. One pilot got hot under the collar because of a delay and got angry at the controller. That irritated me. When I called operations and found out that the pilot was the base commander, I was really bugged. In fact, I lost my cool. I picked up the microphone and shouted over the air for all to hear, "Colonel, you shut up!"

The biggest tragedy of that day, however, was not the words I had spoken in haste and anger, but that the reaction to such a situation was a normal one for me. I had a terrible temper. I was like a bull in a china shop. When things did not go my way, I sounded off. If I was right about something, I let everybody know it in swelling tones.

I had no patience with the mistakes of others. I knew my job and expected others to know theirs to perfection. The more I knew, the angrier I became. What was worse, I could justify my anger in my own mind. I would never have admitted it then, but I can see now that I was a fool.

"He who has a cool spirit is a man of understanding" (Proverbs 17:27).

To understand a person or situation means to
consider what stands under that person or situation.
It is easy to act angrily and hastily simply on the
basis of what we see outwardly without considering
what might be going on within.

Max was a new master sergeant in the squad-
ron. The first day he came to work, he was drunk,
but nothing was done to discipline him. The third
day he was drunk again and had urinated on his
uniform. Still nothing was done. This happened two
or three more times, and still no discipline was
forthcoming. We other sergeants charged into the
commanding officer's room and erupted.

"What is the meaning of this? We demand im-
mediate disciplinary action for Max! Right now!"

Then we were told the inside story about Max.
He was in the intelligence department during World
War II. He was entrusted with top secret information about troop movements. He was captured by
the Germans, and although he was tortured continuously, they could not get the information out of
him.

The Germans also captured his brother and put
them in the same concentration camp. To make
Max talk, they placed the brothers side by side,
kneeling in the camp yard. The Germans put a re-
volver to his brother's head and promised to kill
him if Max did not reveal the secret information.
Max refused. The trigger was pulled and flesh,
blood, and bone from his brother splattered on
Max's face.

When the war was over, Max was released. He
weighed only seventy-five pounds. He spent the
next four years in Walter Reed Hospital under

heavy sedation. By the time he was released, he was addicted to drugs. The government knew that if Max were discharged, he would end up on Skid Row. So they allowed him to stay in the service, knowing that he would get drunk repeatedly.

After hearing the story, our wrath dwindled. We had learned a valuable lesson that day: it is best to seek to understand before we make judgments and allow our anger to build.

Anger Defined

Anger is expressed with two different Greek words in the New Testament (*thumos* and *orge*). One kind of anger is the turbulent, boiling kind (*thumos*). The heat has been building up on our mental "burners" for quite some time, until the lid blows off (we blow up)!

The other kind arises just the same as the former, but we take it off our mental "burner" before the lid blows (*orge*). We don't let this anger simmer for a long time. We go to the source and put out the reason for the anger.

The first kind of anger (*thumos*) starts a brush fire but becomes a forest fire unless it is checked (which would then be *orge*). The first kind is like a wild horse—out of control. The second kind of anger is like a tame one—controlled.

Anger Is Permitted

It is all right to get angry. When guided by reason and patience, anger is the right emotion in many circumstances. The Bible permits it. God had the right kind of anger. The wrath of God is referred to about two dozen times in the New Testament. Without the right kind of anger, bad situations would not be challenged and changed.

It is being honest to admit when you are angry. It is often the kind thing to do to admit to someone that you are angry. Otherwise, he would never know that something he is doing is irritating you.

You are also being kind to yourself when you admit your anger. If you continue to repress the anger, it reinforces itself, gains strength; and finally you blow your top and do and say things that you regret. Even your physical body goes through a traumatic shock when you boil over in anger. We are like human teakettles. The hotter we get, the more pressure gets built up inside. Unless there is an outlet, the top will blow.

Controlling Anger

Anger is a powerful force inside us. The Greek philosophers taught that it was the strongest of all emotions. Proverbs tends to agree: the man who can control his temper and can rule his spirit is better than he who captures a city (16:32).

Anger is the nuclear power within us. We can either harness it for constructive purposes or give it free rein toward destruction. If it explodes, the fall-out devastates those whom it touches. It stirs up strife (15:18; 29:22), exalts folly (14:29), and makes us vulnerable to temptation (25:28).

How can we control this awesome power? How can we provide an outlet for this building up of heat? The Bible gives us some ideas:

1. "Don't let the sun go down on your anger" (Ephesians 4:26*).

This command is just as sacred as that one found in Acts 2:38. It is not an option. Wouldn't it be great if each Christian would remove any anger he had that day when he saw the sunset?

But what can we do to remove that anger? We can go to the person, confess the anger, ask for forgiveness, and seek to understand the *inside* reason for the actions or situation.

Jesus said that if we remember that our brother has something against us, we should go to him and be reconciled before we bring our gifts to the altar (Matthew 5:23, 24).

Face-to-face communication is becoming a lost art in this country. In a survey I took of wives in a congregation, the number-one complaint was that their husbands did not talk with them. Talking is a natural outlet and helps many times to release the feelings of anger.

But be cautious! Do not talk loudly when expressing your anger!

"A gentle answer turns away wrath" (Proverbs 15:1).

When you talk softly, guess whose anger is turned away first. Your own! When I had a temper problem regularly, I noticed that the louder I yelled, the madder I became. One day when I came to work in the control tower, I turned down the volume of all the speakers. What a shock this was to my fellow workers! Whenever I would come to work, the controllers would automatically turn up the volume on the speakers so they would be able to hear the pilots above my screeching. I forced myself to talk softly so the pilots could be heard. What a change that made in my attitude! I discovered that it is awfully hard to really get mad when you are chewing someone out in a soft voice.

"Love your enemies, bless them that curse you, do good to them that hate you, and pray for them which despitefully use you" (Matthew 5:44, KJ).

2. Another God-directed outlet is to turn the power of anger into constructive energy. Jesus was speaking of this principle when He talked about doing good to our enemies. This is such a powerful way to use energy that it fairly melts our enemies. They are unable to handle that kind of power. Doing the unexpected is always overwhelming.

"If your enemy is hungry, give him food to eat; and if he is thirsty, give him water to drink; for you will heap burning coals on his head, and the Lord will reward you" (Proverbs 25:21, 22).

Solomon's advice was the same. Doing the unexpected kindness will cause the enemy to turn in shame.

Not only will this approach help our enemies, it will also help us. Try it! The next time you feel like lashing out at someone, burn up the energy in doing something nice for that person. Take the garbage out for your wife. Fix the screen door or take time to put that handle on the bureau drawer. Fix your husband's favorite meal. That will turn down your burner, and you both will be in a better frame of mind to discuss the issue that irritated you.

3. "A man's discretion makes him slow to anger" (Proverbs 19:11).

Another important outlet is to take the time to look at all sides of an issue before speaking your mind. To use discretion is to evaluate all sides, and also involved in this is exercising patience and long-suffering. We would love each other better if we only understood what each person is going through. Self-control is also a mark of love (1 Corinthians 13:4).

Try to figure out what makes the other person

act the way he does. For instance, when you are behind a slow driver, instead of getting mad, consider the possibility that he may be having car trouble or may be looking for an address in an unfamiliar part of town. When the driver in front of you waits such a long time before pulling out in front of traffic, consider the possibility that he may have been involved in an accident at one time and is traffic-shy.

When a person makes a mistake at work, remember that you make mistakes, too. We all do. When a person lashes out in anger at you, consider the possibility that he may be ill or having a bad day.

When you are starting to blow up because of some irritating situation, ask yourself if this situation is going to make any difference to you in five years. If not, leave it be. In five years, you will not remember the situation, but the person who was the target of your anger may never forget that you lost control of your temper.

Seek to control your temper; don't let it control you. It is better to rule yourself than to capture a city (16:32). I have used that verse to help me so many times. I have learned to control my anger; I feel like a winner in this area of my life, and you can, too! Just cool it!

JUST FOR TODAY

I will try to see all sides of an issue or situation that irritates me. I will not yell. I will resolve my anger before sunset. I will do something kind and constructive for someone who makes me angry.

Chapter Four

Turn From
Temptation *(Proverbs 1:10)*

Temptation is impartial. It comes to the black and to the white, to the rich and the poor, to the college graduate and to the kindergartener, to the Christian and the non-Christian. Even Jesus was "tempted in all things as we are" (Hebrews 4:15).

Solomon emphasized in Proverbs that receiving instruction was vitally connected to resisting temptation. The following chart will illustrate:

Receiving Instruction	Resisting Temptation
Hear, my son, your father's instruction (1:8).	If sinners entice you, do not consent (1:10).
But he who listens to me	Shall live securely, and shall be at ease from the dread of evil (1:33).
My son, if you will receive my sayings (2:1)	Discretion will guard you, understanding will watch over you (2:11).
My son, do not forget my teaching, but	Let your heart keep my commandments (3:1).
Fear the Lord	And turn away from evil (3:7).

Solomon was concerned about the effect that temptation could have on his son, so he gave him much instruction concerning it:

"My son, if sinners entice you, do not consent" (Proverbs 1:10).

"Discretion will guard you, understanding will watch over you, to deliver you from the way of evil" (2:11, 12).

"Do not envy a man of violence" (3:31).

"Do not enter the path of the wicked, and do not proceed in the way of evil men" (4:14).

What Is Temptation?

Solomon instructed his son that temptation, which leads to sin, comes from our own desires. In chapter after chapter he compares the thoughts and motives of the wicked with those of the upright. James also discussed temptation in this manner:

"Let no one say when he is tempted, 'I am being tempted by God'; for God cannot be tempted by evil, and He Himself does not tempt any one. But each one is tempted when he is carried away and enticed by his own lust" (1:13, 14).

The *Revised Standard Version* correctly translates the Greek word "desire" instead of "lust." We are tempted by our own desires.

Some people have tried to escape temptation by suppressing all desire, but that is not the answer. Our basic desires are God-given: hunger, thirst, security, sex, love, etc. These are not evil. They become evil when they are channeled in the wrong direction. God provided us with a wonderful world to satisfy our desires, and He wants us to fulfill our desires in a way that would benefit us, not hurt us. He provided guidelines for meeting those desires.

God is our Creator as well as the Creator of the world; thus He certainly knows exactly to what limits we can go without getting hurt. It is similar to how car manufacturers provide an operator's manual with every new car. The manufacturer knows the car inside and out, and he wants the owner to get the most out of the car. In a similar manner, God wants us to enjoy the wonderful world He has provided for us. To enjoy it fully, we must follow the guidelines He has communicated to us.

God's commands are like guardrails along a winding mountain road. As long as we stay within the bounds of the guardrails, we will be safe as we travel along. If we get outside them, or bump against them, we are headed for much pain and perhaps destruction.

Satan also enters the picture. He knows the God-given desires we have, and he is aware of the availability of the world to fulfill those desires in the wrong way. He also knows the boundaries that God has given us to prevent us from harm. With great cunning he lures and entices us to go beyond the bounds God has set. When we yield to him, we plunge over the guardrails, to our pain and hurt.

The word "entice" describes hunters who imitate the sounds of animals so they can come close enough to the animal to catch or kill it. For instance, the hunter simulates the sound of a duck to encourage the ducks to swarm over the lake. The sound is real to the ducks, but whammo! They get caught. Proverbs tells how the devil entices us:

"Come with us, . . . We shall find all kinds of precious wealth, we will fill our houses with spoil" (1:11, 13).

"With her flattering lips she seduces him" (7:21).

Everyone is tempted by this process. This is what happens when the opening verses of Proverbs are rejected or neglected (1:2-5, 7). Isn't it about time we stood up and declared to Satan that we are not animals to be enticed? We are people of God, renewed by the Holy Spirit. We should not allow our minds to be squeezed into the mold of a destructive and deceitful environment.

Every temptation we face is really weaker than we are. God promises that He will never allow us to be tempted beyond our ability to resist (1 Corinthians 10:13). We are in a battle. The devil and God are both desirous of capturing our minds and lives. The whole book of Proverbs, contrasting the wicked and the righteous, bears this out. It is up to us to decide who will get us eternally. We must manage our lives accordingly, always remembering that He who is in us as Christians is stronger than he who is in the world (1 John 4:4).

Putting It Into Practice

How can we keep the devil from winning the battle? The Bible has the answer.

1. Do not envy sinners. Solomon made this statement to his son time and time again (Proverbs 3:31, 32; 23:17; 24:1). When I was growing up, I could buy a comic book entitled *Crime Does Not Pay*. I went to movies in which the bad guys were shown at their worst. There was nothing to envy.

Today, sin is pictured as being very pleasurable and beneficial, particularly through the mass media. Television programs have us envying and admiring the wrongdoers. Liquor is advertised as the drink of the successful and "with it" people; the disgusting, slobbering persons that liquor turns people into are never shown. Sexual immorality is made to seem humorous and exciting.

We are being lured and enticed daily. Let us as Christians learn to control what enters our minds and the minds of our children. It will be useless for us to say to our children, "Don't envy sinners," if all that they see and hear glorifies sin.

2. Do not associate with sinners. Few people influence us more than our peers, the special crowd of people that we run around with. Solomon knew that we become like the people whose company we keep:

"Iron sharpens iron, so one man sharpens another" (27:17).

Our friends can influence us for good or bad.

Solomon advised his son to remove himself from the presence of a fool (14:7); to stay away from a hot-tempered person, lest he would learn his ways and so be ensnared (22:24, 25); to keep from associating with heavy drinkers or gluttons (23:20, 21); to avoid the fickle (24:21) and the adulterous (6:24).

We are not to be isolationists, but neither are we to become harmonious partners with those whose lifestyles violate our operator's manual (Bible). Several years ago, a young boy was found in a chicken house in the eastern part of the United States. His parents had put him there after his birth. He lived with the chickens for ten years. When he was found, he clucked like the chickens and picked the food off the ground like the chickens. Tragically, that close association had taken its toll on his life.

It is foolish to think that the company we keep does not affect us. Solomon said it so well:

"He that walketh with wise men shall be wise: but a companion of fools shall be destroyed" (13:20, KJ).

3. Before entering into an activity, ask yourself if Jesus would do it if He were in the same situation. If you don't think He would do it, you know that as a Christian you should not do it.

4. Feed upon the Word of God. Read the Bible daily. You cannot know Jesus' thoughts or God's will for you if you do not read His book. Meditate upon it. God's Word will give you strength to fight temptation. The psalmist summed it up:

"Thy word I have treasured in my heart, that I may not sin against Thee" (Psalm 119:11).

Jesus fought the temptations that beset Him in the wilderness by recalling to His mind verses that pertained to the way Satan was tempting Him. The Scripture drove Satan to find another way of temptation each time, and finally he fled (Matthew 4).

Summary

Make no mistake! The devil is after you! He wants to capture you and escort you to the pits of Hell. He uses your God-given desires, and he baits and entices you. Resist him!

"Resist the devil and he will flee from you" (James 4:7).

JUST FOR TODAY

I will seek to stay within God's boundary lines. I will resist the devil and turn from his companions.

Chapter Five

Like Your
Labor *(Proverbs 22:29)*

He was just four years old when he asked, "Daddy, can I help?" I was changing the oil in the car, what I felt was a man's job. How could a little boy help with that? Besides, the car was just a few weeks old. I did not want a little boy messing around with my new toy.

But I knew that the right thing to do as a father was to promote a healthy attitude toward work, and that meant letting him help when he was interested in helping. "Sure, you can help, son," I quickly replied, trying to think rapidly what I could allow him to do. I set him on top of the radiator. The oil intake was just opposite the radiator on top of the engine. I let him hold the oil can with its spout in the hole as the oil poured in. Randy really felt important; I could see it in his eyes.

When it was time to put in the third can of oil, curiosity got the best of him. He slowly picked up the can and tilted his head and the can just enough to see if the oil was really coming out. It was really coming out, and flowing all over that new car engine.

My first impulse was to scream. My second impulse was to send my son into the house. He was going to destroy my new car! But then I got sensible. I knew that every car I have ever owned had eventually ended up in the junkyard. I knew that this new Duster also would end up in the junkyard, while my son would grow up into a young man able to make a contribution to this world, if I handled this situation properly. I didn't want him heading for the human junk heap, so I swallowed my irritation and showed him how to clean up that engine.

As we worked together, I explained to my son the value of putting oil into the car. I'm sure he did not understand all that I said, but he did know that the work we were doing had a reason behind it. We were not just filling up time. I did not pay my child for working with me that day, but I didn't have to. His satisfaction came from doing something that was helpful and needed.

We have added three more children to our family since then, and I have learned that children want to work. They feel important when they can make their own beds and clean their rooms. They feel they are growing up as they do the work they see Mom and Dad doing. They think work is fun. Many people have told me that as children get older their feelings toward work will change. I doubt this, for we have been careful to impress upon our children how their work helps the family, and they derive great satisfaction from that.

Work Attitudes

I am afraid that our nation today is being overrun by people who do not appreciate work, who, in fact, have bitter and hateful attitudes toward work.

This was not the national mentality when I was growing up. World War II started when I was in the second grade. By the time I reached Junior High, I was quite aware of the spirit that pervaded our nation. Men left home to fight, and women went to work. The women worked on the home front to support what the men were doing on the battlefront. They worked to contribute to the country's cause. They worked because the products they made were needed for the benefit of the nation. They took pride in their jobs.

Then the men came home. The war was over. Gun factories were turned into gum factories. We got used to automobiles and nylon stockings. Then television began its bombardment upon our minds. Buy this! Buy that! It was not long until the motive for work was primarily for the pay, so that we could buy *things*. Work was no longer a contribution to fellowman, but a contribution to their selfish desires. Selfishness can destroy a people, and Solomon spoke about this selfish motive for working:

"Do not weary yourself to gain wealth, cease from your consideration of it. When you set your eyes on it, it is gone. For wealth certainly makes itself wings, like an eagle that flies toward the heavens" (Proverbs 23:4, 5).

Anyone who tries to balance the budget knows how money flies out like the eagle!

We know that Solomon was not suggesting that there is anything wrong with getting paid for work, for elsewhere he wrote: diligent labor makes riches, but laziness makes poverty (10:4; 13:4; 14:23; 24:33, 34; 28:19). He was talking about our motives for work. It is one thing to get paid for working, but quite another to work for getting paid.

If pay is our only goal, the product we are working on is just there and we have to put up with it. The service we are performing is simply a duty to drudge through until the eight hours is up each day. Sloppy workmanship results when the workers do not take pride in what they do. Those who are supposed to give service are discourteous, slow, and make it very evident that they don't care a fig about the consumer; they are just there to get the weekly paycheck.

Solomon made a definite effort to instill within his son the idea that becoming skillful at his work was a worthy goal to seek (22:29). Isn't it time that both management and labor took more seriously the contribution their product is making to the life of its users? Isn't it time that people on the assembly line determine to do their very best, simply because a person will use that product and will need it to be flawless? What a better world this would be if each person whose job it is to put a bolt into brake linings were committed to seeing that not one slip by, because someone would need to use those brakes in an emergency. What a pleasant place this would be if each person would determine to give service, true service, to others, not just put in time.

If attitudes toward work would change, then products would not be defective, and services would be performed efficiently. If big business would begin seeking to make contributions to life instead of to their pocketbooks, consumers could trust them instead of being guards and critics.

Management needs to take the time to explain to their workers how their jobs fit into the whole picture of the final product or the service performed. Too many workers have no idea what they are doing. The labor force needs to realize that they are there to help others, not to see how they can goof off when the foreman is not around.

Working for God

Paul wrote to the workers of his day (slaves were paid employees) telling them not to work simply to please the person in charge. He told them to do more than just enough to get by. They should work:

"With sincerity of heart, fearing the Lord. Whatever you do, do your work heartily, as for the Lord rather than for men . . . It is the Lord Christ whom you serve" (Colossians 3:22-24).

As Paul learned (Acts 9), what we do for or against people we are doing for or against the Lord. He is the kind of Father who takes very personally what is being done to His children. When we cut corners or put inferior material into a product that a child of God will use, we are cheating not only our brother, but also God.

God sees our work and takes it personally. Don't think you can please God by praying on Sunday and then do shoddy work or slovenly service on Monday. God deserves better than that. If we are not willing to dedicate our work to Him and for Him in this life, we may not have the opportunity to do so in the next life. How we spend the eight to ten hours a day working is a very important measurement of our stewardship.

The Dignity of Work

God believes in work. At the beginning of time, He worked hard for six days before He rested (Genesis 2:2). He showed us that work was good. He commanded that we work six days a week (Exodus 20:9). That is just as holy and as necessary a command as the command to rest on one day. God wants us to work and knows it is good for us.

It is not enough just to do any kind of work. We all need to do hard physical labor also. Solomon knew this truth long before the American Medical Association advocated it. He wrote to his son, "In all labor there is profit'' (Proverbs 14:23). The word "labor" used here means fatiguing toil. If we would take Solomon seriously, we would have fewer heart attacks and ulcers. How about not buying that riding lawn mower and using your legs another year? How about walking to work, or riding bicycles with your children to the park?

If you can't find enough hard physical work at your house to keep you busy, help some widows or shut-ins in your area. Their yards need cleaning, their houses need painting and fixing up, etc.

Work is so essential for the good of society as well as for the good of our physical bodies that God declares through Paul that a person who will not work should not eat (2 Thessalonians 3:10). God commands that a person go hungry if he does not work. Our nation has pretty well ignored that command. Our welfare offices are crowded with people who *will* not work. (*Note:* I want to make a distinction here between people who *will* not work and those who *cannot* work.)

Solomon said that the lazy man would beg (Proverbs 20:4). Jesus told a significant parable about workers. An employer put many people to work throughout the whole day, even at the last hour of the day (Matthew 20:1-16). The parable was not told to spotlight how wise the employer was to put people to work, but we cannot ignore his deed. He was undoubtedly a Jew who knew the Jewish saying, "He who hath not worked shall not eat."

Why don't we send more people to Washington with that philosophy? When paying jobs are not available in communities, why don't we find and assign work to people rather than paying them for not working? There is much in every community that is not done. Parks need to be cleaned up, potholes in the streets need to be filled, vacant lots need to be mowed, children need recreational programs and leaders, etc.

Solomon also observed that the lazy person is a brother to those who destroy property (Proverbs 18:9). Much of the vandalism prevalent today results because people do not have any work to do. People who don't work do not realize the value of property, so they can destroy it easily without sensing how it hurts others. Those who are lazy are the ones who will litter the streets. They are the ones who will viciously destroy public rest rooms.

We also need to be reminded that any type of work we do is of value and great importance to the society as a whole, unless the work is immoral. We tend to rate people's success according to the kind of work they do rather than how well they do their work. Ditch diggers and construction workers are of just as much importance as accountants or doctors. A janitor is just as valuable in God's eyes as a research scientist. The housewife and mother does just as much to make our world a better place in which to live as the senator and congressman. Work that is done well has dignity and value, whether it is in the grocery store or the corporate law office. God's only requirement is that we do our best.

Putting It Into Practice

What can we do to foster good work attitudes and habits? We must begin at home.

1. Make sure your children do their share of work. Let them know how their work benefits the whole family unit. If they will not work, perhaps they should not eat for a while. Hunger is a powerful motivator.

2. Get out of bed. Solomon emphasized that lov-

ing sleep encourages laziness and poverty (6:8-11; 20:13). Get your children out of bed and give them something worthwhile to do.

3. By your example, may your children learn to take work seriously. Don't talk negatively about your work. Don't scheme and plan about how you are going to shirk your responsiblities on the job. Don't procrastinate or make excuses. Be honest, courteous, and proud of what you do.

4. Wives, realize how your work at home is valuable. Know that all that you do is of the greatest importance, not only to your family but also to God. Since when is it more impressive to say you sell candy at a department store than to stay at home and rear three children?

5. Straighten out your priorities. Know what is of true value and importance and allot your time and effort accordingly.

6. Work alongside your children. Teach them the skills you know. Encourage them in their work, praising and complimenting them often.

7. Don't buy on credit and get stuck with too many monthly payments. Then your only motive for working will not have to be getting the paycheck.

8. Determine how your work is of benefit to others and keep that in mind as you work.

9. Whatever you do, do it unto the Lord. Work for the common good and for the lasting reward.

JUST FOR TODAY

I will determine how my work benefits others. I will do my best in my job and realize that I am working for God.

Chapter Six

Don't Be
a Hermit *(Proverbs 18:1, 2)*

I was a city boy. I could walk to school and to the grocery store. The nearest I ever came to a country life was a plot of weeds near our house. So when my family and I moved to the country three years ago, quite an education awaited me!

Our country home is not a mansion with white fences and beautiful horses in the pasture. In fact, our house is just twenty yards from the road and sits on less than an acre of land. We are squeezed in among several farms. Since we moved here, I have learned to enjoy dabbling in agriculture. I have planted shrubs, trees, and flowers, but I have trouble keeping up with them even in our small yard.

We've decided to leave the raising of animals to those on the neighboring farms. My wife and I have committed ourselves to rearing children instead. Even at that, I have learned many lessons about country life.

We hadn't lived here long when our neighbors, who raise cows and pigs and rear children as well, staged a blessed event—the birth of a calf. That event set me to thinking. That new calf was hardly dry before it was walking on its own. Neither Mother Cow or Papa Bull carried that calf anymore. Yet I've been carrying children in my arms for eleven years now without a break. I'd always thought humans were the most developed of all of God's creatures, so why was there this big difference in the abilities of the new calf and a newborn child?

It dawned upon me that one essential difference between human beings and the creatures of the animal world is the prolonged dependence of one human on another.

Our children were all normal at birth, and each one was totally helpless. Each one's survival did not rest on the "survival of the fittest" philosophy, but upon "survival through dependence." Each child needed and still needs their mother and me; and, of course, we must admit that we have also needed them.

Desire for Independence

But when does this need we have for other humans stop? When do we finally come of age? When are we finally able to make it entirely by ourselves? We expend a lot of energy trying to reach that stage of maturity, don't we?

The two-year-old thinks he has reached this stage. He can't dress himself, can't go to the potty, can't put sentences together, or prepare his own food, but he thinks he is ready to be his own boss. He wants his independence and often demands it.

The teenager also thinks he is ready for his independence. He wants freedom of choice. He would rather act shamefully in front of the "oldsters" in the name of freedom than be *forced* to do anything. Some would rather not work at all, exercising their freedom of choice, than to be squeezed into a successful career through someone else's decision. Some would prefer to wear rags and live in filth as long as it is *their* decision.

Yet a teenager is no more ready for independence than a two-year-old, for many teenagers are almost totally dependent on their peer groups. What their peers think and do become the teenager's Bible. Just as the two-year-old needs Mother and Father to carry him, the teen needs the approval of his friends to carry him.

It seems that we are always searching for that star of independence. Some change jobs often just to prevent feeling tied down. Some divorce their mates to experience freedom and independence. Women, through the women's liberation movement, are standing on the platform of self-determination and the freedom to be themselves. Yet many find that being without a mate is lonely and dreary, even though there is some freedom. Many women are finding that in the daily work force they are not really free. They usually have to take orders from someone and must punch a time clock, as well as caring for the home and family.

Total independence from others is often not possible, and for many of those who do achieve it, it is not a happy existence. Find someone who is totally unattached and has no responsibility for others, and you will find a miserable person. Find a person who is totally selfish, and you will find the person who is most apt to commit suicide or who will commit heinous crimes.

Human beings made in the image of God are not meant to achieve total self-direction or to be entirely free from the influence of others. We are not made to be independent or to have no attachment to others. We are not meant to live entirely apart from others.

Interdependence

The book of Proverbs points out the truth over and over again that we are not meant to be totally independent, but we are meant to live with and for others in interdependence. This is the natural way to live and results in a healthy person—intellectually, physically, emotionally, and spiritually. Proverbs 18:1 states it clearly:

"He who separates himself seeks his own desire, he quarrels against all sound wisdom."

Hillel, one of the great Jewish teachers, advised, "Separate not thyself from the community."

The person who separates himself is the one who refuses to live in a give-and-take relationship with the people around him. He refuses to subordinate his own desires for the good of the group.

Proverbs emphasizes that such a philosophy is against all sound wisdom. Why? Because people are connected to each other, and they need each other. Dependence upon one another is God's design for our survival and maturity. The way we enter into this world is the way we are to continue in this world—needing others. Solomon undergirded what he wrote in Proverbs 18:1 with this parallel truth in Ecclesiastes 4:9-12:

"Two are better than one because they have a good return for their labor. For if either of them falls, the one will lift up his companion. But woe to the one who falls when there is not another to lift him up. Furthermore, if two lie down together they keep warm, but how can one be warm alone? And if one can overpower him who is alone, two can resist him. A cord of three strands is not quickly torn apart."

There is nourishment and strength in the community, but there is malnutrition and weakness in the "loner" approach to life (even the Lone Ranger needed Tonto).

The Church an Example

The church is to be a model of this cooperative interdependence. Paul compared the church to a body in which no member had the right to feel either inferior or superior to any other member (1 Corinthians 12:12-31). A member of the body that decides to function apart from the rest of the body will die. Each member of the body needs the other members for its own survival.

Even though we are individuals, unique and special, we need other individuals to be whole, complete, and healthy. Living in a cooperating fellowship with others is essential to our survival. Paul said that we Christians are connected to the Head of the body, Jesus Christ; but we are *held together* by each other:

"The entire body, being supplied and held together by the joints and ligaments, grows with a growth which is from God" (Colossians 2:19; see also Ephesians 4:16).

How could the infant church described in Acts 2 survive and become the giant church pictured in Acts 28? Partially because the members continued in the fellowship. They did not go off in isolation from each other to learn the apostles' teaching, to pray, and to break bread.

The Corinthian church, which had so many problems, had to be reminded that they were called into fellowship with God's Son (1 Corinthians 1:9). How does one fellowship with God's Son? Certainly *not* by neglecting the body of Christ, which is the church (Ephesians 1:22, 23)!

The Son of God lives in men and women. To neglect others is to neglect Christ (Matthew 25:31-46). Paul learned that truth in a dramatic way. He had been persecuting the church, but Jesus said, "Saul, why are you presecuting *Me?*" (Acts 9:4).

What about you? Have you been neglecting Christ? To neglect the church is to neglect Jesus. To neglect fellowship with the church is to separate yourself from Jesus. That is why immediately after Paul reminded the Christians in Corinth that they were called into fellowship with God's Son, he exhorted them to live in fellowship with each other (1 Corinthians 1:10). Then he spent the rest of the letter telling them how to do so.

Fellowship is the sharing of our lives with and for others. We not only contribute to others but we receive from them as well. Such sharing helps us all to be more complete, mature, and healthy.

Independent Attitudes in the Church

As children of God, we often go through the same struggle for independence as we did as children of men. We seek for total independence at various stages of our Christian walk.

While still "babes," we think we know it all and are ready to be on our own with no help or advice from anyone. We have hardly cut our teeth on the Word of God, when we are ready to stand up and tell the elders where they have gone wrong. Then if things don't go our way, we stay home.

When we are spiritual adolescents, we might be tempted to start experimenting with liberal ethics rather than adhere to a more conservative code. We might cut the apron strings from the church in which we have grown spiritually and begin to float from congregation to congregation and from religious fad to religious fad.

When we feel we have reached spiritual maturity, we can easily begin to think that we have all the answers, that we are the big bosses who have no need to listen to others. It is possible for a church leader to attend every service of the church and still separate himself from the other members. He can make decisions entirely independent of others.

What is the basic ingredient in such independent attitudes? Proverbs tells us it is pride. Pride is being puffed up with one's own self-importance. "Pride goes before destruction, and a haughty spirit before stumbling" (Proverbs 16:18).

The proud person thinks he is so much better than others that he cannot learn from them. A proud person cannot receive the support from others that he needs. Left to himself, he makes wrong decisions and eventually stumbles.

Proverbs stresses many times that we all need to receive advice and counsel:

"Where there is no guidance, the people fall, but in abundance of counselors there is victory" (11:14).

"A wise man is he who listens to counsel" (12:15).

It is the fool who is so stuck on himself that he will not seek or listen to counsel (12:15; 1:7; 1:30, 31). The fool wants to communicate only his own thoughts (18:2), and thus he remains a fool.

Putting It Into Practice

The popular song, "People" states, "People who need people are the luckiest people in the world." How about you? What is your attitude about depending on others? Are you willing to receive as well as give?

Answer the following statements with a yes or no as they pertain to you:

1. I listen to a sermon or lesson for what I can learn, not for what I can find wrong with it.

2. When I am with others, I find myself listening more than talking.

3. Before making a decision, I first study God's Word about the issue. Then I subordinate my will to God's.

4. If God's Word does not specifically spell out what my decision should be, I will talk with others and listen to their advice.

5. Without guidance from others, I believe I can be wrong much of the time.

6. I think I need others if I'm going to "get it together" in this world.

7. I regularly get together with God's people.

8. I attend church faithfully, even when a person other than the minister speaks.

9. I believe I could learn something from a teenager.

10. I read the Bible often because I learn from the written Word.

A "no" answer to many of these would indicate you have a serious problem with your attitude. It is possible to be a spiritual hermit in the midst of a crowded church. Don't crawl into a mental monastery. For the sake of your well-being and health, for the sake of your happiness, for the sake of Christ and His church, recognize your interdependence with others and reap the enormous benefits of fellowship.

JUST FOR TODAY

I will not think that I am right in all my opinions. I will recognize my need for others. I will listen to others in order to learn, not to criticize.

Chapter Seven

TNT—Handle With Care *(Proverbs 18:21)*

Words work. Words result in action, as illustrated on the first few pages of the Bible and in the first few days of time. God spoke and things happened:

"Then God said, 'Let there be light'; and there was light" (Genesis 1:3).

"Then God said, 'Let there be an expanse in the midst of the waters' " (v. 6).

"Then God said, 'Let the earth sprout' . . . and it was so" (v. 11).

"Then God said, 'Let there be lights in the expanse of the heavens,' . . . and it was so" (vv. 14, 15).

"Then God said, 'Let the waters teem with swarms of living creatures' " (v. 20).

"Then God said, 'Let the earth bring forth living creatures' . . . and it was so" (v. 24).

"Then God said, 'Let Us make man' " (v. 26).

God spoke, and a whole universe was created. Then God's Word became flesh (John 1:1, 14) and dwelt on earth. And when Christ (the Word) spoke, nature responded. Diseases were healed, winds were calmed, demons fled, trees withered, and the dead arose.

Our words are not as powerful as God's, but much power is unleashed upon our world through our words. Our words are like living TNT. Nations go to war because of words. Wars stop because of words. Contracts are made through words. Great thoughts and ideals as well as evil, diabolical plots are expressed through words. People become Mr. and Mrs. by uttering words. Later, uttered words may separate them. Words can make the sick well, and the well sick. Friends are made and lost through words. The greatest destructive vehicle on earth lies in the mouth of men. And through man's words, constructive progress and changes are made.

Our words can destroy or uplift another person, both temporarily and eternally (Proverbs 18:21; Ephesians 4:29; James 3:6). What we say can cause another to be saved or can cause one to be lost eternally. Our words can also be a basis for our own salvation or damnation. Jesus said:

" 'For by your words you shall be justified, and by your words you shall be condemned' " (Matthew 12:37).

Some say talk is cheap, but it isn't. It is costly. It can cost a soul, a marriage, a nation, and a destiny. Few things are more important than the words we speak.

Words Reveal Character

Our words reveal who we are. Jesus said:

"The things that proceed out of the mouth come from the heart" (Matthew 15:18).

The longer a person talks, the more he reveals about himself. In fact, it is best to keep your mouth closed until you get your head on straight, as Solomon suggested:

"Even a fool, when he keeps silent, is considered wise" (Proverbs 17:28).

James expressed the same idea when he wrote:

"If any one does not stumble in what he says, he is a perfect man, able to bridle the whole body as well" (James 3:2).

The word "perfect" means "mature" or "complete." A person who can control his tongue has really come of age.

When Peter wrote about the sinless character of Jesus, he included the fact that the words of Jesus' mouth were flawless (1 Peter 2:22). When John saw the vision of the saved in Heaven, he wrote about their pure speech (Revelation 14:5).

What do your words reveal about you? Is your outlook on life negative or positive? Your words will show it. Do you complain or rejoice? Do you argue or are you peaceable?

Are you slanderous or gracious? Are you bitter and resentful, or are you kind and generous? Are you boastful or unassuming? Do you criticize or encourage? Do you threaten or cajole? Do you seek revenge? Do you enjoy gossip? No matter how you try to hide these traits of character, sooner or later your words will reveal the real you.

Words Feed Character

Our words come from our thoughts, but our words also feed our thoughts. We can feed our characters with good nutrition or with garbage, depending upon the words we habitually use.

It is a never-ending cycle. You may criticize another person. That may be a new adventure for you; usually you find the good in people, but this particular person really bugs you, so you tear him down. The more you speak negatively, the more negative thoughts come to mind and pass through your mouth. You begin to enjoy it, and before you know it you have developed a habit of criticizing everyone and everything. Words can poison our thoughts, which will in turn produce more tainted words.

You can also determine to say only nice things. Once you begin and listen to yourself say those kind, positive words, you begin to enjoy how it makes you feel. Before you know it, you have developed a good habit. Yes, thoughts produce our words, and our words mold our thoughts. Solomon made this truth clear:

"A fool's mouth is his ruin, and his lips are the snare of his soul" (Proverbs 18:7).

Evil talk can trap us into evil lives (12:13). James also wrote that the tongue sets the course of our life on fire (3:6). Our words can guide and control our character like the rudder guides a ship (3:4).

Words Affect Others

I will never forget Eileen's story. Her husband had been critically sick and in a coma for days, when the doctor called her to tell her Harry could not make it through the night. Eileen went immediately to the hospital and began the vigil at his bedside, realizing that by sunrise she might well be a widow.

Her mind flashed back over their life together. The memories came flooding back in a rush. She suddenly realized that she had not told Harry recently how much she loved him. She got out of her chair and leaned closely to his body in the bed. She knew he had not responded to any communication for days, but she had to tell him of her love. For many minutes, she whispered into his ear the intimate talk of lovers. When she had finished, Harry had a faint smile on his face.

In the morning, Harry could talk. He could recognize sights and sounds. Five years later, as Eileen told me this story, Harry was watching the football game on television. They were enjoying a full life together.

Most people would say this was a miracle, but as Solomon knew many years ago, there is power in the tongue to heal—or to kill:

"Death and life are in the power of the tongue" (Proverbs 18:21).

This was not just figurative talk. Rash words are like thrusts of a sword, but wise words bring healing (12:18; 13:17; 16:24).

"A soothing tongue is a tree of life, but perversion in it crushes the spirit" (15:4).

A crushed spirit keeps a person from handling sickness well (18:14), but a good word can make a person glad (12:25). A good word works like good medicine.

We are even being told today by some experts that many people actually get sick because of the kind of speech that is directed toward them. Harsh words spread animosities, and animosities cause distraught emotions, and distraught emotions cause many illnesses. We may someday discover that our voices spread more diseases than viruses and stop more sickness than vaccinations.

Let your voice vaccinate people with the medicine of God's grace, for "the mouth of the righteous is a fountain of life" (10:11).

Putting It Into Practice

It is time to take an inventory of your personal speech pattern. Answer the following questions to determine where you need to improve. (Better yet, have your mate or friend rate your speech.)

1. Is my talk bright and sunny, or dark and dreary?

2. Is my talk dirty or pure?

3. Is my talk about myself mostly, or about others?

4. Is my talk soothing to the ear, or screeching and grating?

5. Do I inform with my talk, or do I bore others with it?

6. Is my talk bitter and resentful, or gentle and kind?

7. Do I complain often?

8. Do I compliment others often?

9. Do I contradict others frequently?

10. Do I praise the Lord often?

11. Do I express my gratitude to others?

12. Do I encourage or discourage others?

JUST FOR TODAY

I will meditate upon the awesome power of my words. I will evaluate my speech habits and seek to improve.

Chapter Eight

Tame Your Tongue *(Proverbs 17:27)*

Someone has observed that since we have two ears and only one mouth, God expects us to listen twice as much as we talk. That is not a very scientific statement, but it may have truth in it. Solomon told his son:

"He who restrains his words has knowledge" (17:27).

This does not mean we are not to talk, but it does remind us that we need to listen more. James wrote:

"Let every one be quick to hear, slow to speak and slow to anger" (James 1:19).

This must be an important truth for God to continue to stress it across the years that separate Solomon and James.

It Can Be Tamed

James also wrote that no one can tame the tongue (3:8), but he did not mean it the way it sounds. He did not mean it is impossible to tame the tongue; he meant that no person by himself could tame the tongue.

When the tongue has been touched by the influence of the devil, it becomes poisonous (3:6-8), but the wisdom from above working within a person can change that (3:17, 18). In his earlier reference to the tongue (1:19), James also put the control of the tongue in the context of God's gift from above (1:17).

Paul also taught that the use of the tongue could be controlled. After he wrote about receiving Christ (Colossians 2:6) and being raised with Christ (3:1), he admonished the Christians to put aside abusive speech (v. 8), since we are to consider the body dead to the former things (v. 5). When Paul spoke of our being new creatures in Christ, he warned that we are no longer to let unwholesome words pass from our mouths. Instead, Christians are to encourage and build up one another (Ephesians 4:24, 29). Thus we can conclude that we can control the use of our tongues.

The following paragraphs contain some important and helpful guidelines toward taming our tongues.

Learn to Listen

We need to learn to listen. Two little boys were overheard discussing this principle and how difficult it is to understand.

One boy said to the other, "I can't understand my parents. First they teach me to talk, now they tell me to keep quiet."

The art of listening is as important as the gift of gab. There have been many times when I have not listened to someone who was talking to me. While he was talking, I was planning what I was going to say when he took a breath or paused. Often I would think to myself, "I wish he would shut up. It is my turn to talk." Sometimes I would even interrupt, so I could contribute to the conversation. I've had people do that to me, too. It is very unpleasant.

Do not assume that you know what a person is saying before he has a chance to say it completely. Many times when I have interrupted persons to charge in with my answer, I have fallen flat on my face, just because what I had assumed they were going to say was not what they had in mind at all. Hear the other person out completely and really listen. Don't daydream. You may miss an important point he is making. Ask questions in order to fully understand the person's view. And don't assign motives to a person pertaining to why he said a certain thing in a certain way. You are probably wrong and may be judging a person unfairly. Solomon stressed this point:

"He who gives an answer before he hears, it is folly and shame to him" (Proverbs 18:13).

Think Before You Speak

Many people shift their mouths into high gear without ever getting their minds out of neutral. Solomon wrote:

"The heart of the righteous ponders how to answer" (15:28).

A carefully thought out answer will bring joy to the hearer (15:23). There is more hope for a fool than there is for a man who is hasty in his words (29:20). A wise man does not tell everything he knows (12:23)

Why does a wise person show such restraint? Because he understands that before he speaks he needs to know all the facts and feelings about an issue. If he speaks prematurely, he may reveal his stupidity (17:28).

A wise person also evaluates the situation first to determine whether the hearer is ready to hear what he has to say before he speaks. Jesus did this as He once admitted to His disciples:

"I have many more things to say to you, but you cannot bear them now" (John 16:12).

A wise person also knows that too much talk eventually unearths the garbage in our minds. We are not perfect, and the longer we talk, the more evident our weaknesses are. Solomon spoke to this point:

"When there are many words, transgression is unavoidable" (Proverbs 10:19).

A popular Jewish saying is, "A fool's tongue is always long enough to cut his own throat." So don't be trigger-happy with your tongue; you may shoot off what you will regret.

Refrain From Gossip

Solomon made it clear to his son that tattling will separate close friends (17:9) or even members of a family. I know this is true from my own experience.

I have a twin sister named Knova. Up until a few years ago, I would not be in her presence for very long when she would bring up the fact that I tattled on her all through school. Now, that must have happened thirty-five years ago, but she was still bringing it up for discussion. I can't remember doing that to her, but the important point is that she never forgot it.

Not long ago I asked my mother if I really did tattle on Knova. Mother told me that I couldn't wait to get home from school to describe every detail of Knova's life. Now I understand why Knova and I have never had a very close relationship. It has only been in the past three years that these wounds have healed, but the scars are still there.

For this reason, we do not allow our children to tattle on one another. We want them to grow up being friends and being responsible for each other. James wrote that only a double-minded person (hypocrite) can bless God and curse men with the same mouth (3:9-12).

Few things are as unkind as passing on rumors, whether they be true or false. At times you cannot control the gossip you hear, but you can control the gossip you spread. Once you let the words get past your teeth, you have lost control. The rumor will change, be distorted, and grow all out of proportion. It will soon become a hideous monster unleashed to hurt others.

I once experimented with this principle in a class of twenty students. I whispered in the ear of the first student in the row, "The president went out with his wife last night." I asked him to whisper what he heard to the next student, and so on down the rows. I expected that what I said would be distorted, but not so badly as it was. I was shocked when the last student repeated, "The garbage man didn't pick up the garbage last night." If this could happen to a rumor passing through twenty mouths, just imagine what happens to some of the rumors you tell.

Don't think that you can get away unscathed when you pass on juicy tidbits to others. As you cut down others, you will be digging a pit for your own fall. You may not intend for any damage to be done, but rumors are impossible to control.

When we were first married, a woman called my wife to tell her a story that was intended to hurt her. She said, "I hate to be the one to tell you this,

Julia, but I saw your husband riding through the country with his arms around a woman."

Julia, laughing on the inside, replied, "Oh, yes, that was me. We had a great time!"

Fortunately, we were able to kill that rumor at its source, but usually it doesn't happen that way. *Never* does gossip do any good, it always causes damage. It plants seeds of poison in people's minds, seeds that germinate and spread, and are difficult to stamp out. Determine within yourself not to spread poison.

Talk Positively

Be a bearer of good news. Look for the bright and beautiful things in life and talk about them with others. There are so many dark clouds that blow into our lives, we don't need to add to them. We are all burdened with problems; we don't need to hear more bad news. Proverbs pictures the thought for us this way:

"Like cold water to a weary soul, so is good news from a distant land" (25:25).

While anxiety in the heart of a person weighs him down, a good word can make him glad (12:25). Multiply gladness and spread joy with your words.

There is a saying, "Make your words tender and sweet today, for you may have to eat them tomorrow." Solomon said that sweet speech has healing properties (16:24) and increases persuasiveness (v. 21). Don't yell, demand, gripe, and threaten. Talk tenderly and sweetly instead.

Be Discreet

I grew up believing this little saying: "Sticks and stones may break my bones, but words will never hurt me." As I found out, however, words *do* hurt!

Solomon told his son that the words of a whisperer go down into the innermost chambers of the body (26:22; 18:8). The rash tongue is like a sword that pierces (12:18). Many times the damage done is hard to repair. Thus Solomon warned:

"A brother offended is harder to be won than a strong city" (18:19).

Let us be careful to choose our words and be certain we are not misunderstood. Then we will avoid hurting people.

There are times to take things lightly and times not to. Some people make a joke out of every situation.They come bouncing into the hospital room like they were viewing a circus.

The thought is illustrated in Proverbs this way: singing to a troubled heart is as out of place as taking off your coat on a winter's day or like pouring vinegar on soda (25:20). It is like pouring salt on a wound.

We must learn that at times, silence is golden. Sometimes the best way we can minister to someone who is in need is to be there but not say a word.

Let us determine to speak and to listen as mature Christians should. Let us build up one another with our words.

JUST FOR TODAY

I will really listen when someone talks to me. I will consciously think before I speak. I will seek to spread joy with my words and will stop any gossip I hear.

Chapter Nine

Share the
Wealth *(Proverbs 30:8)*

Does God want you to be rich? A popular philosophy is being spouted these days equating wealth with being righteous. Those self-proclaimed proponents of this idea say that if you have the proper seed faith, you will become materially prosperous. They continue by saying that if you are not prospering, there must be something wrong with your relationship to God. This has caused many Christians to become concerned about their spirituality if they are having a hard time financially.

At the opposite extreme, we also hear that God sanctifies poverty and condemns wealth in any form. The proponents of this philosophy feel that wealth is evidence of spiritual infancy. Jesus' command to the rich young ruler to go and sell his possessions and give them to the poor (Matthew 19:21) is quoted along with His words to the multitudes:

" 'So therefore, no one of you can be My disciple who does not give up all his own possessions" ' (Luke 14:33).

As with many trends in thinking, neither of these positions has developed its stance from the *whole* of God's teaching on the subject, and thus God's balanced perspective has not been grasped and communicated.

The Balanced View

The writer of Proverbs presents God's balanced view, as is evident in his remark:

"Give me neither poverty nor riches" (30:8).

This may seem like an odd request, but Solomon rightly understood that a man's relationship cannot be measured by either what he has or by what he does not have. A man's stance with God is measured by the disposition of his material possessions, not by his acquisition of them.

Both riches and poverty can lead us into temptation (30:9). The rich person can trust more in his material things than in His Creator. He can become greedy and resort to dishonest and violent ways to keep and increase his wealth. The poor person can become so envious of those who have more than he has that he will become greedy and succumb to thievery and violence to obtain wealth. Riches can become his only thought or goal in life. Love for money is the root of all evil (1 Timothy 6:10).

Paul experienced the balanced view in his own life:

"I have learned to be content in whatever circumstances I am. I know how to get along with humble means, and I also know how to live in prosperity; in any and every circumstance I have learned the secret of being filled and going hungry, both of having abundance and suffering need" (Philippians 4:11, 12).

Solomon wanted his son to have the right view of wealth. In the following paragraphs, I will discuss some of his main points.

Riches come from God. Solomon tells us:

"It is the blessing of the Lord that makes rich, and he adds no sorrow to it" (Proverbs 10:22).

Solomon did not mean that all we have to do is sit back and watch wealth rain down upon us. "Money does not grow on trees," as the popular saying goes. In this same context, Solomon made it clear that the person who puts aside laziness and enters into diligent work can become rich (10:4).

But the person who has worked hard for his wealth must never think that the riches he enjoys are simply the result of his own sweat and blood. Such independent arrogance blinds a person to being appreciative of anything or anyone. In the movie "Shenandoah" the plantation owner illustrated such arrogance. At mealtime his prayer went something like this: "God, I planted the seed, I plowed the ground, I cultivated the crop, I harvested the grain, I put the food on the table, but I thank You anyway."

God is the possessor of all things; therefore, any riches gained call for our recognition of the real source—God. I am happy to say that some of the most appreciative people I know are those who are the wealthiest.

Poverty does not come from the devil. It may seem logical to some to conclude that, since riches come from God, poverty must come from the devil. Solomon does not offer that as a conclusion:

"The rich and the poor have a common bond, the Lord is the maker of them all" (22:2).

The rich and the poor should look at each other as fellow creatures of God. God is the Maker of both; thus both should live with each other as brothers, not as competitors. Differences in income should make no difference in the way God feels about us. He loves us all.

There is a prevalent teaching in some circles

that poverty is a sign of unrighteousness. If this is true, how can we explain the poverty of Jesus' family? The offering that Joseph presented at Jesus' purification was what a poor person would give—two birds (Luke 2:24). The normal offering was supposed to be a lamb, but God allowed the poor to give other offerings (Leviticus 5:7-11).

If poverty means a person is not blessed by God, how can we explain that Jesus had no place to lay His head and had to be buried in a borrowed tomb? How do we explain that people of faith were poor (Hebrews 11:37, 38)?

If poverty is a mark of God's disapproval, why were so many people in the New Testament church poor (Acts 2:45; 11:29; 1 Corinthians 1:26; 2 Corinthians 11:27; 8:2; Romans 15:26; Galatians 2:10; James 2:5; Revelation 2:9)? Using all common sense, we must admit that neither riches nor poverty is linked to spirituality.

Riches are not God's confirmation of the rich. Just because a person is rich does not mean that God puts His stamp of approval on the person's character or activities. A person can gain wealth illegally, but the individual or his family will not profit in the final analysis (Proverbs 10:2; 13:11; 15:27). He will not gain any treasure in Heaven. Thus Solomon told his son not to envy the sinner (23:17), nor desire the delicacies of a selfish man (23:6).

Solomon felt it was better to have "a little with righteousness than great income with injustice" (16:8). A man's bank account says little about his spiritual account. So it will do no good to make material possessions our goal as a means to gain confirmation from God. God's blessings fall as rain upon both the good and the evil (Matthew 5:45).

Farms owned by the Mafia can experience bumper crops as well as those owned by the most pious.

Man should not make material rewards his delight, but should delight in God's righteousness instead. It is better to eat stale crackers in a house of love and peace than to eat leg of lamb in a house full of bitterness and strife (Proverbs 17:1).

Generosity is a virtue. Above all, Solomon wanted his son to know how to share whatever he had. Someone has said that the greatest gift you can give to a rich man is advice on how to be generous.

There are three basic attitudes that a person can have about material wealth. One is, "What is mine is mine, and I'm going to keep it." This type of attitude is for the loser. The person who hangs on to what he has will be in want himself (11:24).

Jesus illustrated this truth in His parable about the rich man and Lazarus (Luke 16:19-31). The parable has three parts: (1) the rich get richer, (2) the poor get poorer, (3) the rich and poor change positions. The rich man's wealth increased and he lived in daily splendor. Lazarus longed to eat the rich man's garbage, but even that was denied him. He got so weak that the dogs began licking his sores. But when the two died, their positions were reversed.

The rich man became the beggar, and Lazarus lived in a luxurious place of plenty. The rich man begged the Father to send Lazarus from the dead to warn his brothers, "lest they also come to this place of torment." What did he want to warn his brothers about? Not only that there was a place of torment, but that they must learn to share their riches, or they would remain in eternal want.

Another attitude about wealth is, "What is yours is mine, and I will take it." This is the philosophy of thieves, and is condemned. Robbery can be done with a pistol or a pencil. One of the injustices of our day is that the intelligent thief who uses his pencil to cheat, exploit, and embezzle is thought of to be "high class," while one who breaks into a store is thought of as "scum." God does not make such distinctions. To Him the white-collar crook is as evil as the shirtless crook.

Solomon wrote grave warnings about white-collar thieves, such as false scales (Proverbs 11:1; 20:23). Some people bribe others to land a contract. Solomon spoke against that as well (15:27). Dishonesty, an evil of society, is strongly condemned.

The third attitude about wealth is, "What is mine is yours also, and I will share it to meet our needs." Solomon wanted his son to have this attitude. Sometimes this attitude is expressed by selling goods to a person who has a need. Solomon condemns a person who stockpiles needed goods to force the price up (11:26).

More often the attitude is expressed by giving. Some people simply cannot afford to buy what they need. In Acts 2 and 4, Christians sold their possessions to share with poorer Christians (2:45; 4:36, 37). This does not mean they sold *everything*. They still owned houses (2:46). This was not a form of communism as we know it today. They were voluntarily sharing. They had the gift of giving with liberality (Romans 12:8).

Such sharing pleases God. The person who shares will get richer (Proverbs 11:24):

"The generous man will be prosperous, and he who waters will himself be watered" (v. 25).

God will reward the generous (22:9). In fact, Solomon pointed out that anytime we are being generous with the poor we are making a loan to God, and God will repay us (19:17). Think of that! You can make a loan to God! The saying that "God is no man's debtor" is not true. God wants our loans, and He will repay us with interest.

Solomon told his son to use his wealth to honor God (3:9). If we can honor God with our use of the material things He gives us, it will not be ill-spent. What does it mean to honor God with our wealth? Solomon said:

"He who oppresses the poor reproaches his Maker, but he who is gracious to the needy honors Him" (14:31).

Note that he says "gracious," not humiliating.

The only offerings spoken about in the New Testament had to do with helping the poor (1 Corinthians 16:1; Romans 15:26; 2 Corinthians 8, 9; and Philippians 4:10-20). Paul made it clear that helping the poor would honor God (2 Corinthians 9:11-14). Jesus put it this way:

" 'To the extent that you did it to one of these brothers of Mine, even the least of them, you did it to Me' " (Matthew 25:40).

That is why Jesus will repay us. He even said that when we invite the poor to dinner we will be repaid at the resurrection (Luke 14:12-14). What an exciting thought! Think what it will be like in Heaven when Jesus says, "I want to thank you for making me a loan on earth, and now I want to repay you."

Putting It Into Practice

How much of your giving is designated for the poor? Who has been at your house for dinner lately? Each Christian should give a portion of his offering to someone in need. The Jews had a saying: "Greater is the alms-giver than the bringer of sacrifices." The person who helped the needy was greater than the one who brought bulls and lambs for the ritualistic ceremonies.

Is your money being used to operate a building or to help people? Oh, you think I'm stepping on your toes too hard? Paul's advice to Timothy was quite clear and strong:

"Instruct those who are rich in this present world not to be conceited or to fix their hope on the uncertainty of riches, but on God, who richly supplies us with all things to enjoy. Instruct them to do good, to be rich in good works, to be generous and ready to share, storing up for themselves the treasure of a good foundation for the future, so that they may take hold of that which is life indeed" (1 Timothy 6:17-19).

Do you want a good foundation for the future? Then invest in the poor. Do you want to have a part of "life indeed"? Then share with the needy (Proverbs 17:5; 19:17; 22:2).

JUST FOR TODAY

I will thank God for my material possessions and will designate a portion of my giving to someone in need.

Chapter Ten

It's a Family Affair *(Proverbs 1:8)*

We all want to be successful, but what makes it happen? What makes us worthy of honor by our fellowmen and termed a success in life? For what will we be most remembered when we leave this life? When do we make a contribution to our society?

Some time ago, I read an airline magazine article entitled "How to be a Successful Executive." The article included advice from five of the top executives in the nation. Tragically, all of them mentioned that the one thing that had to be sacrificed in order to become a top executive was the *family*.

Many people in our society seem to believe that to be successful and great in any field, we have to work, work, work, from dawn till dawn, and rush, rush, rush from meeting to meeting. We cannot take the time to meet the needs of our families if we are to become successful. Our commitment has to be a one-way commitment: to our jobs (so they say and live).

God does not abide by that philosophy and never has. He always has taught that a successful leader would also take his family responsibilities seriously. After God told Abraham he would be great, He told Abraham how his success would come to pass:

"I will bless you, and make your name great" (Genesis 12:2).

But Abraham's success would not be at the expense of his family. To the contrary, Abraham was chosen so that he would teach his family the way of the Lord and be a good example of high moral conduct (18:19).

We cannot read very much of the book of Proverbs without being impressed by the fact that King Solomon followed that same route to success. Solomon was a great man. He was a politician, a builder, a merchant, a prophet, and a writer. He wrote three thousand proverbs and more than a thousand songs. He was knowledgeable and wise. He spoke of botany and biology. People came from all over the world to listen to Solomon (1 Kings 4:32-34).

It would have been easy for such a great man to be so busy giving advice to everyone else that he would have no time to advise his own children. But his children did not have to eavesdrop on his public sessions to gain guidance for their lives. Solomon did not speak and write just for the general public. In fact, we know very little of what he said to his clients, his soldiers, his fellow politicians, and his architects. But we know a great deal of what he said to his children. So the politicians and those of the business world will have to eavesdrop on Solomon as he advises his son to receive great counsel from a sharp mind.

Much of Proverbs was written by a very busy man to his son. Solomon was not interested in ruling the world if it meant he would lose influence over his own son. He was a master in sharing himself. That is why we read the phrase "my son" over and over again (Proverbs 1:8, 10, 15; 2:1; 3:1, 11,

21; 4:10; 5:1, 20; 6:1, 3, 20; 7:1; 19:27; 23:15, 19, 26; 24:21; 27:11). Solomon could often say, "Do not forget my teachings" (4:2) because he spent much time teaching his son. He could have delegated the responsibility to someone else, but he did not.

Taking the Time

We will not be able to say to our children, "Don't forget our teachings," unless we are teaching them. Unfortunately, in our nation today most intellectual and practical skills are taught to our children in a place *outside* the home. The public school teaches our children to drive cars, cook, sew, do carpentry work, and to raise crops and cattle. Our Sunday schools and youth programs teach our children about our religious faith. I'm not saying that this outside education is bad; it is not. It is valuable. But I am distressed that the home is almost entirely left out of the child's education. Parents are not consulted about the programs or the curriculum. It is not long before the values and beliefs of the home are neglected and ridiculed. Perhaps this has happened because parents have become too lazy, too unconcerned, or too busy.

Teaching our children means we must spend time with them. We teach, not just with our mouths, but also with our lives. So we must commit *time* to our children. I don't buy that little saying, "It's not the quantity of time you spend with your children; it is the quality of time that is important." That is just a rationalization we parents use for spending a minimum amount of time with our children and a maximum amount of time with our careers, recreation, and hobbies. Our children aren't sure what we mean by "quality time," but they do know that they need a large *quantity* of our time. It takes time to do things with children that they will cherish and remember.

Just as I was writing this, I decided to take a break and go upstairs. As soon as Randy, my ten-year-old, saw me, he said, "Daddy, will you wrestle with me?"

My first thought was, "I want to rest." Then I thought of all I had to do to finish this chapter and get ready for my college classes that started the next day. But then I thought of what it meant to my son if I would give him a little of my time and attention.

What would a person think if he walked into our family room and saw a forty-three-year-old college professor wrestling on the floor with a ten-year-old boy? Who cares? My son cared more than anyone else. I am convinced that the time we spend doing things with our children on their level makes all the difference in the world as to our effectiveness in teaching them.

In his book, *Help, I'm a Layman,* Ken Chafin illustrated the significance of doing little things with the children. He came home just in time to hear the evening news, when his five-year-old daughter asked, "Daddy, will you be home tonight?"

"No, I've got to go speak to some people about what a good father ought to be." He then asked her to think and to whisper into his ear what she felt being a good daddy meant. As she did, he wrote down her advice:

> To catch a fish
> To build a fire
> To fly a kite
> To catch a butterfly
> To plant a flower
> To get a kitty out of the mud

All of those little things take time. Our children need *us* more than all the material *things* we give them. Think back in your childhood. What do you remember about your parents? Don't you remember and cherish the times they shared themselves with you?

My wife clipped a comic strip out of the Sunday paper that illustrated this point very well. It went something like this:

Ditto is standing in front of his dad's desk and asks, "Dad, could we play ball together?"

"Sorry, son. I have to get this report done."

"When you finish, could we shoot the BB gun together?"

"Sorry, son. Then I have to take your mother shopping."

"How about when you get back?"

"No, I have to mow the yard."

Alone at his desk, Hi says to himself, "That boy has to learn there is more to life than play."

Walking dejectedly down the hallway, Ditto thinks, "I wish Dad would learn that there is more to being a daddy than making excuses."*

We have a definite responsibility to teach our children, to give them guidelines toward self-discipline, nurture them in the way of the Lord, to share our faith with them. Our teaching will be most effective and have the most influence on their lives if we show them how much we care and if we give of ourselves and our time.

Your Turn, Kids!

The child-parent relationship flows both ways. Solomon continually reminded his son of his re-

---

*From *Hi and Lois*, by Mort Walker and Dik Browne.

sponsibility to receive and obey his parents' teaching:

"Hear, my son, your father's instruction, and do not forsake your mother's teaching" (1:8).

"Receive my sayings, and treasure my commandments within you, make your ear attentive to wisdom, incline your heart to understanding" (2:1, 2).

"Do not forget my teaching, but let your heart keep my commandments" (3:1).

"Let them [wisdom and understanding] not depart from your sight; keep sound wisdom and discretion" (3:21).

"Give attention that you may gain understanding, . . . do not abandon my instruction" (4:1, 2).

Each child is to commit himself to live out the godly teaching of his parents and thus honor them. A child honors and respects his parents when he carries on their teachings:

"A wise son makes a father glad, but a foolish son is a grief to his mother" (10:1).

A foolish child actually brings about the destruction of his parents (19:13). The lives of many a parent have been wrecked with the worry, sickness, and bitterness of a broken heart caused by their children. It is a disgrace for a child to do that to his parents (19:26).

A child gives his heart to his parents when he delights in their ways (23:26), but he humiliates them when he adopts a lifestyle inferior to theirs (28:7). Children should bring blessing and honor to their parents, not grief and bitterness through foolishness (17:25). For any child to curse his parents by the way he talks or lives is to live in darkness (20:20).

Sometimes children have a hard time appreciating rules that the parents enforce. They seem to think the parents don't trust them, so they make up rules. No, that is not the case, kids! Your parents simply don't trust the world out there. They don't trust the "Joe Blows" who could harm their children. Not long ago, a seven-year-old rode his bicycle to the store one block from his home. He did not return. He was found stabbed thirty-eight times and thrown onto the railroad tracks. Children, be thankful that parents love you enough to make some rules for your safety.

We grown-up children must respect our parents also. That respect may involve seeing ourselves as our parents see us. My mother does not see me as a teacher, writer, or preacher. Whenever I visit her she says, "Son, you should eat more. Son, you need to wear a heavier coat."

When Mother was in the hospital recently, I drove four hundred miles to be with her. Would you believe what she said to me when I arrived by her hospital bed?

"Son, did you remember to lock your car?"

I have learned not to be irritated at that, for it has dawned upon me that, no matter what, I will always be my mother's boy. Likewise, my son always will be my boy. If he should become President of the United States, he will still be my boy. Should he decide to make a tour to Russia, I'm sure I would call the White House (collect) and tell him to take a heavy coat because it is cold in Russia.

Jesus was speaking to grown men when He said, "Honor your mother and father" (Matthew 15:4). We never outgrow that command. This two-way parent-child relationship is so important that Jesus came to earth to restore it. The last words from the prophet who looked for the Messiah were:

"And he shall turn the hearts of the fathers to the children, and the hearts of the children to their fathers" (Malachi 4:6*).

The Challenge

Much of Proverbs reflects a father who loves his son enough to teach him, and a son who respects his father enough to listen.

Let us sit at the feet of Solomon as if we were his children and apply to our lives his advice. For his advice to us is really our heavenly Father's advice to us. How we listen to it and apply it reflects our honor to God. His sharing it with us through Solomon reflects His care for us. It is a family affair!

JUST FOR TODAY

I will take the time to teach and be with my children. I will take the time to write or tell my parents how much I appreciate them.

Chapter Eleven

Decide to Discipline (*Proverbs 3:12*)

"I'm fed up with the system. I love teaching, but I cannot take the classroom anymore. The teachers are afraid of the principal. The principal is afraid of the superintendent. The superintendent is afraid of the parents. The parents are afraid of their children. But the children are afraid of no one. It is an unbearable situation." With those words, a teacher resigned.

It is not a complicated process. If we fail to discipline our children, we will have undisciplined children. Undisciplined children, sadly enough, become undisciplined adults, and this becomes an unbearable situation. We Christians must decide to have discipline in our families, both at home and in the family of God at church.

In more than a dozen different passages, Solomon wrote to his son about discipline in a direct way. Indirectly, however, the whole book of Proverbs is disciplinary in nature. Discipline refers to directing, guiding, or teaching a person. It does not always include punishment, but it may.

The Essence of Discipline

We believe in discipline when we are raising plants. We take great care to make sure the plants get the right start and have the right basis for their growth. We aerate the soil, using plant food, and using fertilizer. We make sure the seeds or small sprouts are placed in just the right kind of soil and in just the right spot to receive the proper amount of light. We give the plants every opportunity to grow strong by watering them often and by pulling out the weeds that threaten them. We know how important the right kind of environment is for their growth. We spare no expense, time, or effort if we really believe in having hardy, beautiful plants.

We use all these principles of preventive discipline when raising plants; but we must use the same care, effort, and time to provide the proper environment and encouragement for the growth of our children as well. We must be sure they receive godly teaching every day as the proper basis for their development. We must provide them with proper companions and seek to weed out the threats to their character. We must be sure that we model the proper example of conduct and character.

We will be models or examples of living, whether we plan to or not. Just yesterday, I walked into the family room where Julia, my wife, was reading a book. I said, "Hi, babe," and leaned over and kissed her. Within seconds, our nineteen-month-old Rachel scrambled up the side of her mother's chair, said "Hi, babe" and immediately puckered for the kiss. We are always teaching by who we are and what we do.

We also have to use corrective discipline when raising plants. Often young sprouts need a small wooden stake or some type of support in order to grow straight instead of growing lopsided or crooked.

We have a redbud tree in our front yard that the wind evidently had bent over almost double before we moved here. It would not have been very pretty if we had allowed it to continue to grow so crookedly. I propped up its trunk with a long board for more than a year to make it grow straight. I used corrective discipline on that tree. What a shame it would be if I used it on the tree, but not on my children!

Children are no more capable of deciding how they should grow than a tomato plant is capable of deciding how it should grow best. Children need guidance and support. They need to know when they err and need help when making decisions. When we rebuke (or reprove) them, withdraw privileges, or use physical punishment, we are showing our love for them. We are showing them that we want them to take the right path and grow straight and true.

Solomon wrote that the withholding of discipline would result in the destruction of our children and is an indication that we hate them (Proverbs 13:24; 19:18). To discipline is to rescue our children (22:15). We will not kill them with punishment (23:13), but they will die without it (15:10).

Principles of Discipline

To make certain we are administering discipline in the proper way for our children, let us consider these important principles.

1. *Explain the value and purpose of discipline.* Solomon did not just punish his son or just enforce the rules. He told his son about the purpose of such guidance. He explained that discipline was an act of love. How tenderly Solomon said it:

"As the Lord reproves those whom He loves, so a father reproves the son in whom he delights" (3:12*).

Solomon was saying, "I discipline you because

I am delighted in you. You are a very precious person to me. I care enough about you to help you develop properly."

We always have told our children that we discipline them because we love them. I can remember times when I have had to spank three at a time. But before doing so, I always explained that I loved them so much that I wanted them to grow up properly. I would tell them what kind of persons they would be if I allowed them to continue in the way they were going.

Children appreciate explanations. They may not always understand the words, but they can understand the loving, caring attitude of the parent who is uttering the words.

Our son enjoys riding his bicycle into Carterville, a small town a few miles from our home. But we have a rule: he cannot go by himself. He did not like the rule at first or understand why it had to be. He trusts everyone and could not imagine anyone wanting to hurt him. He also feels he is terrifically strong and would have no trouble taking care of himself on a remote country road. But the rule has stuck, and he is beginning to realize that we made the rule out of our concern for his safety.

Solomon said that he who listens to reproof acquires understanding (15:32), so be patient. Your children will eventually understand your attempts at discipline.

My wife amazes me with her insistence that an explanation coincide with an act of discipline. Even when our children were very young, she disciplined with a firm "no," an explanation, and a smack on the hand. As they began to creep around on their "reach and destroy" missions, she was always there with her firm explanations of why they should not do something. They could not understand her words, but they grasped her tone and knew they were being disciplined.

Solomon wrote that whoever loves discipline loves knowledge (12:1), but that can be true only if knowledge (explanation) accompanies discipline.

2. *Have a positive attitude.* Don't destroy your child's self-image with overbearing, negative discipline and attitudes. Compliment and praise your children often.

We even compliment our children on the way they handle disciplinary measures. We tell them how proud we are of the way they accept our teaching. Yes, they were wrong in what they did, but if they took the punishment in the right spirit, we praise them for it.

If you call the children stupid, dumb, or clumsy, they will begin to feel like failures. If you yell and scream and say they will never learn to do right, they will soon give up trying to do right. All children have foolishness bound up within them (22:15), but they should not be made to feel they are total failures, with no hope of improving. Doing wrong as a child is simply a part of growing up, experimenting, and learning, trying to find out the right way to live.

Solomon approached the discipline of his son in a positive manner. He said that a wise son would accept his father's discipline (13:1). The son would then have a goal of being wise and strive to achieve it. Solomon wrote:

"He who regards reproof will be honored" (13:18).

The son who wanted that honor would seek to live in such a way that he would deserve it.

3. *Vary the form of discipline.* Many people

seem to think that Solomon's talk of using the "rod" of discipline (22:15) means that a switch or stick is the only godly way we can discipline a child. Using a stick to administer punishment as the *only* mode of discipline is a bad mistake.

The word "rod" was a common word used for any form of punishment. When God used *men* to correct others, he called those men a rod (2 Samuel 7:14). God's *mouth* is called a rod (Isaiah 11:4). When God used a *nation* to punish another He called that nation His rod (Isaiah 10:5). A corrective *experience* was called a rod in Ezekiel 20:37. *Troops* were called a rod in Micah 5:1. In fact, strong discipline was referred to as a rod of iron, not a rod like a wooden stick (Psalm 2:9; Revelation 2:27; 12:5; 19:15).

To say that Solomon meant to use a literal stick when disciplining is totally unfounded. When Solomon spoke of the rod of discipline, or correction, he meant any form of correction that fits the occasion. In correcting a child, sometimes a look is all that is necessary. At other times, a clearing of the throat, a raising of the eyebrow, or a snap of the fingers is all the rod that is needed. Often we use our mouths as a rod when we utter a rebuke, a reproof, or counsel. The rod could be the removal of some privileges for a time. The rod can be the hand as well as a yardstick, ruler, or a hairbrush, applied to the seat of the pants. So don't think that a literal rod or stick standing in the corner of a room in your home is going to solve all your disciplining problems.

Discipline in the Church

Not only has God given us the responsibility of rearing the children we have begotten or adopted, but also of rearing the children He has begotten and adopted. God wants His children to be directed toward the goals that are pointed up in these Scriptures: Colossians 1:27, 28; Ephesians 4:15; 2 Corinthians 3:18; Philippians 1:9. Thus, discipline is needed in the family of God.

Alexander Campbell said that discipline in the church is as essential as its doctrine (*Millennial Harbinger,* Vol. VI). Campbell also said:

> "To cut off an offender is good; to cure him, is better; but to prevent him falling, is best of all. The Christian spirit and system alike inculcate vigilance in preventing; all expedition in healing offenses; and all firmness in removing incorrigible offenders."

—The Christian System, p. 69

Paul's letters are disciplinary in nature. When he commends, rebukes, admonishes, teaches, and builds up, he is disciplining. In some of his letters, he directly calls for stern disciplinary measures. He even suggested that some people needed to be isolated from the fellowship before they would change (1 Corinthians 5; 2 Thessalonians 3:6-15; 1 Timothy 1:20; Romans 16:17; Titus 3:10).

This type of punishment may seem farfetched to us today, but it would be good discipline if the fellowship in our churches were such that when a person is absent he really misses something. It would be similar to the feeling one gets when he is away from home and knows he cannot hop in the car and go back when the rest of the family is there for a special occasion. All of a sudden he appreciates home and family more. So it should be in the church family. The church member may be made to realize what he is missing and come to appreciate the fellowship of the Christian family more than ever before.

This punishment of isolation was advocated so that the sinning person would be led to repentance (2 Corinthians 2:5-7). It was done as one brother helping another, not as two enemies in a war (2 Thessalonians 3:15). It was done to prevent a disastrous spread of sin (1 Corinthians 5:6, 7). It was done to prevent the Christian from having a false sense of comfort and security or having the idea that God overlooks the continuation of his sin.

When we discipline someone in the church, we must do it for him, not against him. We must do it to detour him from destroying his spirit. It is to be done only when all other approaches fail, and it is apparent that the person will not respond to other methods (Matthew 18:15-17).

Let us discipline one another, build up one another, and direct each other to an eternity with God. Let us discipline because we love and because we care in both our physical and our spiritual families.

JUST FOR TODAY

I will discipline my children. I will praise them often and discuss with them why I discipline them.

Chapter Twelve

Marvelous Marriage *(Proverbs 5:18)*

An eight-year-old boy was watching his mother fill out a job application. He was rather bored with the whole experience. Suddenly his mouth dropped open and his eyes grew large. His mother had just written an "F" next to the word "sex" on the application form. The boy exclaimed, "Mom, you flunked sex!"

Then the mother's mouth dropped open and her eyes grew large. She thought to herself, "How did my son know that word?"

It is easy for us to become uncomfortable with any mention of sex in any context. Who thought up this "sex stuff" anyway? It did not come from the mind of a dirty old man. Sex was designed by our heavenly Father, and God has said a lot about the subject.

For some reason, we think it is "Christian" to leave the subject of sex out of our teaching and our study of what God has said on the subject of sex. Perhaps we think that people who need guidance in this area will stumble upon the appropriate passages in the Scriptures. Quit dreaming! People don't usually stumble upon the teaching of other subjects, so why do we take such chances?

Happily, some Christians are beginning to "take their heads out of the sand" and discuss sex. A few years ago, A Christian Continental Congress on the Family was conducted in St. Louis, Missouri. Five books recorded the sessions of that meeting, and of the five, one was entitled *The Secrets of Our Sexuality*. I am pleased, for God said much more about our sexuality than about many of the other topics that were discussed at that meeting.

What Is Sex?

Sex is your whole being, not just a part of you. God made us male and female (Genesis 1:27). I am a male from the top of my head to the bottom of my feet. It is an error to restrict a person's sex to certain parts of the body.

Between Husband and Wife

Solomon wrote more about the sexual expression between husband and wife than any other writer of the Bible. He gave some godly-inspired advice to his son when he wrote:

"Let your fountain be blessed, and rejoice in the wife of your youth" (Proverbs 5:18).

The word "fountain" referred to the man's wife, the source of his children. The husband is to see to it that his wife is happy (blessed) sexually. Making her happy begins by his rejoicing in her.

Solomon made sure his son did not misunderstand his meaning, for he continued his advice:

"Let her breasts satisfy you at all times; be exhilarated always with her love" (5:19).

"Exhilarated" in the Hebrew language literally means "intoxicated." In other words, the husband should be enthralled, infatuated, delighted, elated, excited, entranced, and enchanted with his wife's love.

Solomon expanded this practical advice in his other writing, The Song of Solomon. I encourage all of you husbands and wives to read this small but very important book of the Bible. Some scholars have tried to drain the book of its practical beauty by suggesting that it is really talking about Christ's love for the church, but the book has simply recorded the love and the loving conversation between a man and wife. It illustrates how God intends every marriage to be sexually.

Compliments and endearments flow back and forth between the husband and wife:

" 'How beautiful you are, my darling, how beautiful you are! Your eyes are like doves' " (The Song of Solomon 1:15).

" 'How handsome you are, my beloved, and so pleasant!' " (v. 16).

Nowhere can we read more tender expressions of love than in chapter 7 of this book:

" 'How beautiful are your feet in sandals, O prince's daughter! The curves of your hips are like jewels, the work of the hands of an artist' " (v. 1).

" 'Your two breasts are like two fawns, twins of a gazelle' " (v. 3).

" 'How beautiful and how delightful you are, my love, with all your charms!' " (v. 6).

" 'I am my beloved's, and his desire is for me' " (v. 10).

This is what is meant by being exhilarated with each other. How long has it been since you talked like that with your mate?

Oh, you think such a discussion has no place in a book like this? Remember, I have been quoting from the Word of God. The fact that sex is talked about in this way in the Bible should make clear to us that sexual intimacy in marriage—as God intended it—is not dirty and evil. More of us parents should sit down with our children and describe how beautiful sex can be between a husband and wife, as Solomon did for his son.

Sexual Perversion

Not long after Christianity began, Christians began to think of sex as something dirty and taboo. Most pagan religions included sexual perversions as part of their religious rituals, so it was not unusual for those who were converted to Christ from these religions to associate any sexual intimacy with evil. It was even taught that a husband should not physically touch his wife.

Such a teaching was prevalent in the church at Corinth, so some Christians wrote to Paul for his advice on the subject. In answer, Paul shattered that wrong kind of thinking:

"Now concerning the things about which you wrote, it is good for a man not to touch a woman. But because of immoralities, let each man [husband] have his own wife, and let each woman [wife] have her own husband" (1 Corinthians 7:1, 2).

The word "have" was the common word to denote intercourse.

The dirty connotation to sex was still being taught by some to the extreme that marriage was forbade entirely (1 Timothy 4:3). But Paul considered that teaching to be from "deceitful spirits and doctrines of demons" (4:1).

The writer of Hebrews made it clear that sexual intimacy within marriage was honorable and clean:

94

"Let marriage be held in honor among all, and let the marriage bed be undefiled" (13:4).

The writer assumed that the marriage bed followed a marriage. But when would the marriage bed be defiled? When it was tainted by fornicators and adulterers (13:4). The Greek word for "fornicators" is *pornos,* which denotes immorality, or sexual perversion.

Sexual Intimacy

Sexual intimacy is not only normal between marriage partners, but it is also necessary. Here are some *Biblical* reasons:

1. *For the conception of children.* God blessed Adam and Eve and said to them, "Be fruitful and multiply" (Genesis 1:28). One of the ways He blessed them was by equipping them with the ability to reproduce. But this is not to be the only reason for sexual intimacy. It is not anti-Scriptural for a couple to prefer not to have children, but it is anti-Scriptural for them to withdraw from sexual intimacy for that reason.

2. *For the spiritual protection of each mate.* The mass media makes a grave mistake when it broadcasts the idea that sex is physical only. Sexual intimacy also has emotional and spiritual dimensions to it.

To engage in sexual intimacy with your married partner is a spiritual service. It is one way to protect him or her from the attacks of Satan. Paul made that clear when he told Christians to stop depriving each other (1 Corinthians 7:5). That is a clearly inspired command. If a Christian withholds sexual intimacy from his or her mate, that person is disobeying that command. In the phrase, "except by agreement," the Greek word for "agreement" is *symphonon,* from which our English word "symphony" comes. It describes sounds that blend together in harmony. Paul was saying that a husband and wife can abstain from sexual intimacy when that decision is made *together,* in a blending, harmonious way. In simple language, that means one mate should not repeatedly say, "I'm too tired," or, "I've got a headache."

Deprivation of sexual intimacy must be a mutual decision and for the reason of devoting yourselves to prayer (7:5). Perhaps Paul meant for the prayers to be for the bettering of the marriage relationship. Perhaps the people needed a spiritual retreat occasionally to renew their relationship with each other.

The abstinence, however, is meant to be temporary. Paul warned them to come together again "lest Satan tempt you because of your lack of self-control" (7:5). Sexual intimacy is a spiritual service to both partners in a marriage. God made us to be sexual. Those who have sexual passions are to marry (7:9). Marriage is the God-given environment for expressing our sexual desires, with which God created us. Satan will move in to tempt us if we deprive one another, so let us protect the eternal security of our mates.

3. *For the completion of each mate.* God made us needing each other. We need our mates for the completion of ourselves, unless we have the gift of celibacy (1 Corinthians 7:7-9). We need our mates for affection and love.

Paul said that the wife does not have power over her own body, but the husband does; likewise the husband does not have power over his body, but the wife does (7:4). He meant that neither person has the ability to satisfy himself or herself. You need your mate and your mate needs you. Satisfy each other.

4. *For the release of tension.* Pressures, tensions, and anxieties build up within us much in the same way that steam builds up in a teakettle. An outlet or escape is needed. One of the outlets God provides for us is that of sexual intimacy.

In Genesis 24, we read of Isaac who had much anxiety because his beloved mother had died. God provided an outlet for his anxiety:

"Then Isaac brought her into his mother Sarah's tent, and he took Rebekah, and she became his wife; and he loved her; thus Isaac was comforted after his mother's death" (v. 67).

What a beautiful expression of what sexual intimacy can mean!

5. *For unity between mates.* Sexual intimacy is meant to be an outward manifestation of unity. It also solidifies the unity between man and wife. It is a great act of communication, which is essential in maintaining unity. The Bible often refers to this as "knowing" your mate (Genesis 4:1; Luke 1:34; Matthew 1:25, KJV or RSV) and as becoming "one flesh" (Genesis 2:24; 1 Corinthians 6:16).

6. *For pleasure.* God made sex for our enjoyment. Sex is part of the abundant life Jesus spoke of. Sarah was ninety when God told her she was going to get pregnant. Imagine experiencing morning sickness for the first time at ninety years of age! Can't you just see the looks on the clerks' faces when Sarah came through the check-out counter with a shopping cart full of Pampers! Can't you see Abraham in his bifocals counting the minutes between the labor pains? What a sight it would be to watch Abraham, at one hundred years, leading his

pregnant wife into the hospital's admitting area and asking, "Will Medicare pay for the nursery as well?"

Sarah got the word that she was to have a baby. What was her reaction? She laughed. Why? Because she was old? That was surely part of it, but the main reason was what she herself intimated, "After I have grown old, shall I have pleasure, my husband being old also?" (Genesis 18:12).

Her laugh was evidently a gleeful chuckle. She knew what would have to take place between her and Abraham if she were to get pregnant, and she described it as "pleasure," a word that often referred to intercourse in the Hebrew tongue. Yes, this type of sexual intimacy was what God intended for us.

But Sarah would not have responded in such a manner if her husband had not been a thoughtful, considerate husband who related to her sexually with her needs in mind and not just his own. They must have had a great personal relationship during the day and over the years to have had such a pleasurable relationship at night.

It is important for us to know that successfully satisfying intimacy is not accomplished by getting into bed in a certain way at night, but by how we get out of bed in the morning and how we treat each other during the day.

God created sex for our satisfaction and happiness in marriage. It is one necessary ingredient for marriage to be as marvelous, as exciting, as wonderful an experience as God intended.

Putting It Into Practice

Here are some practical suggestions for enhancing the sexual part of your marriage:

1. Read some Christian books on the subject: *Intended for Pleasure,* by Wheat; *The Act of Marriage,* by LaHaye; *Sexual Happiness in Marriage,* by Miles.

2. Go out on a date occasionally, just you two.

3. Go on a honeymoon for a few days at least once a year, just you two.

4. Tell each other "I love you" often.

5. Keep clean and sweet-smelling.

6. Discuss your sexual feelings and desires.

7. Teach each other what you like during intimacy.

8. Do whatever you can to make sure that you do not always go to bed "dead tired."

9. Help each other with the household chores and work that must be done before retiring.

10. Reserve time each day for just you two to be alone and converse.

11. Read The Song of Solomon and practice saying some of those sweet things to each other.

12. Compliment each other often.

13. Remember the words in Proverbs and rejoice in each other.

JUST FOR TODAY

I will thank the Lord for my mate. I will seek to meet his or her sexual needs as well as other needs.

Chapter Thirteen

Abhor
Adultery (Proverbs 2:16, 17)

How exciting it is to be a parent and to watch my children face new challenges and experiences each day. But it is also frightening! I get this sinking feeling as they embark on their journey in life. It is as if they were adventurers journeying into a vast and unfamiliar territory. I don't want them falling into potholes in the road or getting lost in vast crevasses in the rock. I don't want them to wander aimlessly upon the immense stretches of time. I want them to be well equipped with maps, charts, and strength of character so they can face the challenges of the unknown. I want them to know the temptations that face them, so they can dodge them and strengthen themselves for the many onslaughts that life will shower upon them.

We are hearing a lot about sex and adultery via books, magazines, movies, and television today. We even receive step-by-step directions in how to "have an affair" without getting caught, or having "open marriages" in which either partner can "swing" as he or she wishes. Our children are exposed daily to such wrong and hurtful ideas. Surely we want to expose them equally to the rules God has for their sex lives! Let's quit shaking our heads and begin talking with our children before it is too late!

Oh, you can't find the right words? Well, for

some ideas, let's give a listen to what Solomon told his son.

Adultery Is Tempting

Everyone can be tempted to commit adultery. Solomon spent a great deal of time preparing his son to meet the temptation of adultery. Even though his son was reared with good values, Solomon knew this would not keep the temptation away. Even the finest spiritual families experience the pain of one of its members faltering in the face of sexual temptations. Temptation is universal. Don't think your children will escape it. They may have the strength to withstand such temptations, but they will surely be tempted. This should not alarm you, for temptation is common to all. There is no need to feel guilty when tempted.

Because of the way Solomon advised his son about sexual temptations (Proverbs 5, 6:20 ff., 9:13-18), the son knew that he was not to feel guilty or ashamed about the sexual passions that burned within him. He could retain his good self-image and realize that temptations would always come. He would be prepared for the fiery darts when they came, and would have the strength to deal with them properly. He would know what the guidelines were and what the results would be if he did not follow them.

It is important to know that, even though such temptations will surely come to all people, we do not have to face them alone:

"God is faithful, who will not allow you to be tempted beyond what you are able" (1 Corinthians 10:13).

God does not tempt us, but He does control the

temptations. He never allows Satan to tempt us beyond our present spiritual capacity to resist. Anytime a temptation comes to your mind, you can know immediately that you are bigger than it is or God would never have permitted it.

Solomon talked about temptation with his son with this same positive attitude. Just as surely as temptation will come, you have the power to overcome it (Proverbs 5:1; 6:23, 24; 7:1-5).

Adultery Is Pleasant (Temporarily)

One of the modern philosophies is "how can it be wrong if it feels so good?" We need to be prepared for the lure and enticement, so we will not be carried away by it.

Solomon did not try to hide the temporary pleasantness of sexual sin. He made sure his son knew its attractiveness, so he would not be overwhelmed by it. Solomon admitted:

"Stolen water is sweet; and bread eaten in secret is pleasant" (9:17).

Sexual sin looks and feels so good, but remember the hook that is hidden:

"But he does not know that the dead are there, that her guests are in the depths of Sheol" (9:18).

Don't be fooled by appearances. A destructive time bomb can be wrapped in the most delightful package possible. Worms can live in delicious-looking apples. A cracked block can be under the shiny hood of a brand-new car. Sin can look and feel good, but it leads to pain and destruction.

Adultery Is a Gradual Lure

Solomon outlined for his son the steps a member of one sex might use to gradually lure a person of the other sex into an adulterous relationship. Such a clear disclosure would be sure to help his son keep his eyes wide open and help him avoid getting into a situation that would be difficult to get out of. Here are some things to watch for:

1. *A Lonely Woman or Man* (Proverbs 7:10, 19). The temptation can begin when a mate is away from the presence of his or her mate for a time. The lonely person looks for companionship. The situation can get out of hand and uncontrollable so soon. Caution must be exercised, for loneliness or absence from one's mate can make some people extremely vulnerable to this temptation.

2. *The Wrong Clothing* (7:10). What we wear can give off signals that we never intended. Be cautious about your dress. Do not draw people to you because of what you wear or how you wear it.

3. *Sweet, Sensual Talking* (7:15; 6:2). Most adulterous situations that I know about started through conversation. The give-and-take of listening and talking can draw people very close together. It feels good when someone really listens to what you have to say. It is exhilarating to have a discussion with someone who agrees with you and admires your mind.

Conversation can begin quite innocently between casual acquaintances or between friends; but unless caution is exercised, feelings may arise that extend beyond the boundaries of friendship. Husbands and wives can protect themselves from this pitfall by establishing better communication at home.

Sensual talk (7:5, 16-18) is especially dangerous. When sensual, flirtatious things are brought into the conversation, stop the conversation and leave the presence of that person. Danger is lurking.

Sensuous thinking results in sensuous talking, which can lead to sensuous action. Don't let another's words act as a magnet drawing you into sin.

4. *Secrecy* (7:19, 20). Secrecy and the secure feeling that no one will know what happens lead many to go beyond God's guidelines. It is difficult to resist sexual implications when you are assured that no one will ever know. Very few people enter into an adulterous relationship thinking it will be the subject of the talk around the table at home or in the office lounge at work the next day. Be assured, however, that God knows you sinned and you know you sinned. That is enough.

5. *Flirting Eyes*. Solomon knew about the magnetic attraction of eye-to-eye contact, and he wanted his son to know about it and avoid it:

"Do not . . . let her catch you with her eyelids" (6:25).

A Jewish saying goes like this: "The harlotry of a woman is in the lifting up of her eyes, and it shall be known by her eyelids." Don't suggest thoughts to another with your eyes. If someone sends messages to you through the eyes, turn away.

6. *Touching*. There is something powerful and extremely personal about touching one another. There is not anything wrong with friends touching, but we must be careful. In our society, it is probably better for us to keep our touching to the minimum. It is *why* we touch, *how* we touch, and *what* we touch that causes temptations to flourish. Solomon clearly illuminated the approach of the sexual temptation:

"With her many persuasions she entices him; with her flattering lips she seduces him. Suddenly he follows her" (7:21, 22).

Solomon did not have to worry about the unknown territory his son would face, for his son would know the dangers and darkness that lurked behind the brightness and glitter of the enticements. His son would never be able to use the excuse, "but I didn't know what was happening till it was too late."

Positive Guidelines

Solomon not only spotlighted the pitfalls along the road to show them up for what they are, but he also established helpful, positive principles for his son to follow, principles that would guide and strengthen him, maps to guide his journey.

1. *Establish close family ties* (5:15-17; 10:1-5; 22:6). When love and trust teams up with healthy communication in a family, the children tend to want to live up to the values and ideals of the parents. Solomon gave assurance that his teachings were valuable:

"Keep my commandments and live, and my teaching as the apple of your eye" (7:2).

Are our teachings clear, honest, simple, and about the things in life that really matter? Are our teachings about the sexual temptations our children will have to face? Let us be specific!

2. *Control your thoughts* (6:25). Solomon knew that the way to his son's actions were his thoughts. Jesus referred to the same principle when He said,

"But I say to you, that every one who looks on a woman to lust for her has committed adultery with her already in his heart" (Matthew 5:28).

Jesus meant the type of looking at another for

the purpose of lusting or desiring. It is one thing to notice how attractive a person is, but it is quite another to harbor thoughts about the person's body in a lustful way.

We can control our thoughts, and we must. If desire begins to burn within you, turn away. Go and busy yourself with another activity.

3. *Stay away from bad situations* (Proverbs 5:8). If you don't want to get burned, stay away from the fire. Some people are excited by the lure of temptation. They edge closer and closer, not intending to yield, but just wanting a peek or a little taste of the temptation. That practice is so dangerous. It would be as dangerous as trying to see how close you can get your car to the edge of a cliff without going over. Who can tell what the limit is?

When you are in an uncomfortable situation, see the danger signs, and feel the sensual desire building within you, get away from there and from that person. It is a wise person who will run from danger.

4. *Satisfy your mate sexually*. It was in the context of resisting an adulterous relationship that Solomon advised his son to take care of his sexual responsibilities at home (5:15-17), and to be exhilarated with the love of his wife (5:18, 19). If the sexual relationship between the husband and wife is healthy, then the temptations for outside relationships are so much easier to resist.

Results of Adultery

The father's teaching to his son would not be complete without the inclusion of what results from an adulterous relationship. Adultery ends in hurt and death (2:18, 19) and bitterness (5:4, 5). It is an insecure relationship (5:6); it pricks the conscience

(5:11-14) and leads to ruin. It is destructive (6:32) and disgraceful (6:33). It reduces a person to a thing to be used, not to a human being who is loved (6:26). The naive do it, not the intelligent (9:16).

Adultery Is Sin

I cannot close this chapter without making clear that the Bible considers adultery to be a grave sin which will lead to eternal destruction (1 Corinthians 6:9; Galatians 5:19; Hebrews 13:4). To commit adultery is to neglect your covenant with God (Proverbs 2:17). It is time that people begin to take their marriage vows as seriously as they seem to want to take their destiny. Solomon's ancient advice is still up-to-date:

"Can a man take fire in his bosom, and his clothes not be burned? Or can a man walk on hot coals, and his feet not be scorched? So is the one who goes in to his neighbor's wife; whoever touches her will not go unpunished" (6:27-29).

Of course, there can be forgiveness and cleansing when repentance and commitment to a new way of life are evidenced (1 Corinthians 6:9-11). Christ can give you the strength to overcome any situation. Learn to live within His will and Spirit.

"As you therefore have received Christ Jesus the Lord, so walk in Him" (Colossians 2:6).

JUST FOR TODAY

I will not allow myself to yield to sexual temptation. I will not act, look, or think in a sensual way with anyone but my mate.

CONCLUSION

To live out the principles of Proverbs is really to live out the character of God. That is why Solomon said that respect for God is the place to begin (Proverbs 1:7).

The best living model for putting Proverbs into practice is Jesus, who came demonstrating the character of God to us all (John 1:18; 14:9). Why was He able to do so? The answer is two-fold: power and commitment. On the one hand, He was conceived of the Holy Spirit (Matthew 1:20)—the *power*. On the other hand, He was determined to obey God (John 5:30; 12:49)—the *commitment*.

We cannot expect to be able to put the principles expressed in Proverbs into action by any other path than the one Jesus took. We also need to be conceived of the Holy Spirit. We can do so by turning our lives over to Christ, by believing in Him, and by repenting of our way, changing to do things His way. We can bury our old way of doing things in baptism and at the same time put on Jesus (Galatians 3:27). We will then be raised with Him (Colossians 2:12) to walk in a new way of life (Romans 6:4). That new life receives its power through the Spirit (Acts 2:38; Romans 7:6; 8:2, 8-10).

We put on new selves, and our minds are renewed (Ephesians 4:23, 24). We are born again and have become new creatures (2 Corinthians 5:17; John 3:3-5; Titus 3:5). As in our physical lives, growth must follow birth. We seek to grow into Jesus' likeness (Ephesians 4:15). This is a daily process (2 Corinthians 4:16) and involves commitment (1 Peter 2:2) to learn to live as Jesus would have us live (Philippians 2:8).

When our every thought and deed reflects Jesus' obedience to God's way (2 Corinthians 10:5), we will be utilizing the power that is available to us to live out the principles of Proverbs.

To do so is to be wise. Solomon asked for wisdom (2 Chronicles 1:7-10), and wisdom was the one thing he wanted for his children (Proverbs 1:2-9; 3:13-26; 5:1; 7:4; 9:1-6, 10-12). Wisdom, as the word is used in the Bible, means putting into practice God's morality. And with wisdom comes everything worthwhile: healing (3:8); happiness (3:13, 18); profit (3:14, 15); long life (3:16); pleasant life and peace (3:17); eternal life (3:22); security (3:26); sweet sleep (3:24); freedom from worry (3:25); confidence (3:26); and an honorable reputation (3:35). As Jesus said:

"If you know these things, you are blessed if you do them" (John 13:17).

Read and reread the book of Proverbs, then put the principles into practice, which will delight and honor our heavenly Father.

Having read the entire book, you may want to cut out the following page, which lists all thirteen commitments, and keep it posted as a daily reminder to you to continue putting them into practice.

JUST FOR TODAY

1. I will try to put God's health program into practice by being good, by being joyful, by watching my speech, and by not worrying.

2. I will enrich my mind with what I read, see, and hear. I will remove anything from my environment that would not enhance my Christian life.

3. I will try to see all sides of an issue or situation that irritates me. I will not yell. I will resolve my anger before sunset. I will do something kind and constructive for someone who makes me angry.

4. I will seek to stay within God's boundary lines. I will resist the devil and turn from him.

5. I will determine how my work benefits others. I will do my best, realizing I am working for God.

6. I will not think that I am right in all my opinions. I will recognize my need for others and will listen to others in order to learn, not to criticize.

7. I will meditate upon the awesome power of my words. I will evaluate my speech habits and seek to improve.

8. I will really listen when someone talks to me. I will consciously think before I speak. I will seek to spread joy with my words and will stop any gossip I hear.

9. I will thank God for my material possessions and will designate a portion of my giving to someone in need.

10. I will take the time to teach and be with my children. I will take the time to write or tell my parents how much I appreciate them.

11. I will discipline my children. I will praise them often and explain why I discipline them.

12. I will thank the Lord for my mate. I will seek to meet his/her sexual needs.

13. I will not allow myself to yield to sexual temptation. I will not act, look, or think in a sensual way with anyone but my mate.